It's Me, Not You

Key to Healthy Relationships

Laura McPherson, LPC, LMFT

REAL Influence™
A Foundation for Healthy Relationships

Name: Laura McPherson, LPC, LMFT
Title: It's Me, Not You: Key to Healthy Relationships
By Laura McPherson, LPC, LMFT
ISBN: 9781952369582
LCCN: 2021905891
Subjects: 1. Religion/General
2. Religion/Christianity/Personal Growth
3. Religion/Christianity/General

Cover Designer: Krystine Kercher
Photo Credits: Page 146

Published by EA Books Publishing, a division of
Living Parables of Central Florida, Inc. a 501c3
EABooksPublishing.com

Dedicated to all who value the effort it takes to learn about and help make healthy relationships happen.

Acknowledgements

Ben, you have encouraged, supported and uplifted me along this journey. You are a blessing.

Thank you to The New Dimensions, Agape, and Young Mom's classes at Kingwood United Methodist Church for helping me refine the REAL Influence™ material.

Appreciation goes to all the attendees and their feedback during the REAL Influence™ programs. I am grateful for the different perspectives and suggestions offered.

The FUN (Fellowship, Understanding, Nurturing) Bible study are long time encouragers and prayer warriors for me.

My Live Write Texas tribe supported me with their prayers, encouragement, humor, and suggestions.

Open Hearts Ministry in Grand Rapids, MI provided the venue and care for some of the early changes I had to make to become who I am today.

The protégé program at the Advanced Writer Speakers Association and the National Speakers Association Academy provided mentors, and valuable workshops and programs.

Publishing this book is a direct result of the support of my family, friends, and associates, who prayed, loved, and encouraged me along the way. This group effort kept me going. You all are the best!

Table of Contents

Endorsements

In her new book *It's Me, Not You: Key to Healthy Relationships*, author Laura McPherson challenges her readers to "do better." Her expertise and experience as a counselor bring authenticity and credibility to her writing. In this time of social media, developing genuine relationships can be difficult. We see the highlight reels of people's lives and think we know them. Seldom do we endeavor to do the necessary work to gain and maintain healthy relationships. Laura paints a clear picture of how to achieve healthy relationships, encouraging each person to take responsibility for their own actions. Her insight prompted me to look within and evaluate how I will approach new relationships and how I can do better in current ones. Readers will benefit from the substance this book delivers. Congratulations Laura, you have motivated us to reexamine how we look at relationships. Inspiring us to look deeper, and to develop a clearer vision of why we behave the way we do.

Evelyn Johnson-Taylor Ph.D. Author, Speaker, Theology Professor

When we release a resentment, we are free to reflect on how much energy we spent on it and where this energy could be better spent." This statement alone is worth the investment in *It's Me, Not You*, a new book from Laura McPherson. But she goes far beyond this encouraging word and aids her reader in how to do it—and how to prevent its' return. Written from her view as a licensed marriage and family counselor, Laura discloses her experience with a myriad of examples created from her years in practice. But she never exempts her own learning and shares first-hand understanding of how healthy relationships are possible to achieve. The author speaks to her reader without the dialogue of the mental health professional she is, but as one who has been there herself. This is a must read for those seeking to (finally) take ownership of creating and stewarding healthy relationships in life.

Deb DeArmond, award winning author on marriage and family. Life coach

As the father of three adult sons, I reflect on the time, effort, and energy required to help them grow from boys to men. And not just any men; I wanted them to become men of God. It was, at times, a long and winding road. Laura McPherson's new book, *It's Me, Not You* would have been tremendously valuable during that process. My wife and I realized during those years the boys struggled at times with what we expected from them. Her quote of Brandon Sanderson that "Expectations are like fine pottery. The harder you hold them the more likely they are to crack" is priceless. Laura's insight on this topic provides a gentled path. Other's perspectives and opinions deserve our listening ear and consideration. I'm grateful for the expanded knowledge this book provides and will use it when coaching, counseling as well in my personal life.

Ron DeArmond, coach, men's ministry leader, and author

Laura McPherson's "It's Me, Not You" book is something everybody can benefit from reading because we all have relationships that need to change with only one person being motivated to make that happen. Laura's focus on helping the readers see the power they all have to change the relationships around them by focusing on themselves is profound! And powerful. What a blessing it is to apply these REAL techniques to create healthy and rich relationships in the way God intended for us all. Laura offers such hope to all relationships.

Quinn Kelly, Licensed Marriage and Family Therapist, Renew You Podcast host

Laura's heartfelt writing is a true expression of her highly skilled abilities as a seasoned professional counselor and her profound wisdom as a spiritual teacher. In her book, "It's Me, Not You: Key To Healthy Relationships," she incorporates her original REAL Influence material on healthy relationships into a larger perspective that could help anyone struggling with relationship issues. Her writing provides powerful medicine for anyone concerned with their marriage. It will be a worthy addition to any marriage.

Jim Trenchard, MA, Licensed Clinical Social Worker, Therapist

Laura McPherson has written an important and impactful book that I highly recommend for anyone struggling with relationships. She is an excellent therapist and has now made her wisdom and experience available to a wider audience. Scripture makes it clear that we are "wired for connection"; yet so many struggle with how to keep those connections healthy and affirming. Her book "It's Me, Not You" provides an effective and empowering model based on the REAL Influence™ material she developed and has successfully used in her own work as a Christian counselor and highly regarded speaker. I hope that fellow therapists will add this book to their libraries and encourage their clients to do the same.

Anne Palmer, MA, Licensed Professional Counselor

It is Me, Not You: Key to Healthy Relationships, is a God send to humanity. As a spiritual director who also practices medicine this book is a resource to assisting clients, family, and you in attaining and maintaining wholeness as Christ desires. This book demonstrates authority, experience and results that are clear and concise for all readers who want personal wholeness to live in community with others with healthy relationships.

"When Jesus saw him lie, and knew that he had been now a long time in that case, he saith unto him, wilt thou be made whole?" (John 5:6 KJV)

Laura, like Jesus, saw so many hurting and is offering an opportunity to be healed and enjoy a life of wholeness.

Karynthia Glasper-Phillips MDiv, PA-C

Laura McPherson is a respected relationship counselor. In "It's Me, Not You," Laura uses her professional expertise and her authentic Christian faith to challenge the reader to seek REAL freedom in relationships. I found myself stopping and pondering Laura's words on every page – this piece of writing is impactful. The reader is invited to search for non-productive relationship strategies that have become unhelpful habits in their own life. We are encouraged to find freedom through reachable, practical steps as we learn to leave those habits behind and thrive in REAL community. This book not only shakes us from our relationship complacencies, it supports us as we learn new strategies towards understanding ourselves and each other. It feels like Laura is in the room with us as we read, gently encouraging us to make better choices. Does it take effort to have healthy and thriving relationships? Yes, and the reader will find realistic and achievable methods to apply the principles offered in this inspiring work. Read this book and expect to be changed for the better!

Sharon Tedford, international speaker, singer songwriter, recording artist and founder of 61 Things Ministry

Laura is passionate about helping others learn how to relate in a healthy way. It has been a joy to have Laura speak at various women's events and lead workshops at our church. She always encourages and challenges participants to enter into their personal story so that they may break the chains of the past and embrace a new future. Her new book, "It's Me, Not You," embodies her REAL principals that, when personally applied, are life changing. Her book is inviting, informative, and also challenging. "It's Me, Not You" is a must read for those who want to learn how to relate to others in a healthy way.

Reverend Judy Tefteller, Kingwood and Onalaska United Methodist Church

It's Me, Not You based on the acronym REAL is an enjoyable must read for those of us who have ever stood there with arms outstretched wondering "What did I do"? The author had me examining why I do what I do and considering why others react the way they do. With the examples of real-life situations, I have learned to look inside myself to improve my relationship skills by instinctively examining what effect my words will have on others and on myself. Utilizing REAL's information will greatly reduce the time spent scratching your head and wondering "What happened?

Carl Colmenares, Business Owner

Laura made it so easy to understand how to achieve and influence healthy relationships. I'm blessed to be in relationship with many people even though there have been changes since my husband died. *It's Me, Not You* uses the REAL Influence™ material to help me sort out the things I need to do to keep my relationships healthy. I encourage readers to become familiar with her strategy and make your relationships better!!

Lou Ann Masters, Teacher

Laura McPherson has been a successful counselor for 18 years. She has shared REAL in several settings. Although her audiences are diverse, the participants have benefitted greatly from Laura's REAL Influence™ seminars. Laura uses compassion, insight, humor, and her faith to develop a practical, realistic strategy that anyone can use to understand and deal with the relationships in our lives.

Readers of *It's Me, Not You* will be led through these strategies by reading about issues which shape our relationships or scenarios that portray real life. The steps that Laura takes the reader through are non-threatening and will not overwhelm anyone or point a finger of guilt. These steps are like tools for daily life.

Reading *It's Me, Not You* will give you new insight into how to deepen or strengthen relationships, keep or repair a relationship, or how to respond to an unhealthy relationship. It will lead you to the realization that you are the one who holds the power to shape the health of your relationships.

Genie Pearce, Retired Reading Specialist and Classroom Teacher

We have known Laura for years and have worked with her in a variety of ministry roles. She's a thoughtful, engaging and articulate leader and speaker. We've seen REAL at work among diverse groups and in some very different settings. Whether it be a classroom teaching environment or an intentional workshop. Laura's delivery of REAL's core tenants in *It's Me, Not You* resonates with audiences, readers, and opens doors to greater understanding and nurturing of important relationships and healing when those relationships are in fact broken.

Perhaps the most powerful example of REAL's impact is its role in Laura's teaching at Oaks of Righteousness. The residents at this transitional living house for ex-offenders meet with Laura each week for 3 months to discuss the important elements of healthy relationships with each other, their co-workers, and their families. Many of the women come from dysfunctional families that have strong resentments, unrealistic expectations and no communication. Each week, the residents learn to communicate with each other resulting in less frustration, arguments, and conflict resolution. The principles learned in the REAL program are supported with scripture as lives are transformed and minds renewed. We are thankful for Laura's dedication to the recovery program at Oaks of Righteousness.

Reading *It's Me, Not You* will have you saying at the very least; "I wished I knew this, years ago," or "now I know why that happened." It's quite likely it can unlock a new awareness of how best to nurture, sustain, and repair those relationships that are most dear to us.

Beth Whittier, Director, Oaks of Righteousness
Richard Whittier, Lay Leader, Kingwood UMC

I've had the privilege to have Laura as a mentor as well as working closely with her for several years. Laura's commitment to helping her clients and those around her live the best version of their lives is evident in everything she does. Her REAL Influence™ material found in *It's Me, Not You*, sums up Laura's belief that through healthy connections, we are able to live a more peaceful, authentic life. Instead of a routine workshop on healthy relationships, Laura modeled what genuine connection looks like. I walked away with a better understanding of the ingredients necessary for achieving healthy relationships. This helped me as clinician, and also as a wife, mom, and daughter.

Maryanne Walker, MA, Licensed Professional
Counselor

The REAL Influence™ material found in *It's Me, Not You* is simple, learnable and profoundly effective in experiencing life and relationships that are honest and open. Having personally applied the principles to my life, I believe I have benefitted with genuine loving relationships with family and friends.

Jadi Meyer, Life & Ministry Groups Director

Preface

What is the back story that led me to where I am today? Growing up, I learned quite a bit about loyalty. My father was an Air Force general and our country was experiencing the Cold War with Russia. Loyalty to our country was high on the list for most Americans. As I grew a little older, *loyal* is probably the word I would have used if someone asked me to describe a healthy relationship. Realistically, I probably wouldn't have been asked the question. Questions or comments about healthy relationships weren't normally asked or commented on like they are today. If they were, they weren't in the culture I was living in. When I was in my forties yes, but not when I was young.

Change came during the mid to late 1960s. In the hippie era, healthy relationships were important and took on new meaning. There was more freedom in relationships, there were communes and the need for marriage wasn't as important as in the 1950s. I believe the word loyal was still the word I'd use to describe a healthy relationship. I was a late bloomer in this area. Things personally started to change in my forties. And did they ever.

By all appearances, I was a "put together" woman. I had several leadership roles in our community, married to a man with a job others envied, and children who were smart and athletic. A perfect family or, more accurately, the appearance of a perfect family.

I gradually realized the unacknowledged problems in my marriage were taking a toll. As a young bride, I was told to stay loyal and never talk negatively about my husband to anyone. I never looked any deeper until a crisis and then serious problems emerged. Yes, there was a burp ten years prior, but it came and went. I'm loyal and I will stay the course.

In the late 1990's, my husband and I visited my parents in Virginia. My dad was in a skilled care facility. He had surgery several months before for cancer of the sinus. It didn't look good; he wasn't gaining his health back. I remember saying, to my husband, "I think I am losing the two most important men in my life." And eventually, I did.

My new life was tough, but just the right people were put on my path. I was surrounded by new friends who chose to live relationally healthy. I was plopped down in their midst. I knew I was being taken somewhere I needed to go. I had to keep going. This taste of healthy relationships was like food to a starving person.

I realized I needed to examine and change some of my thought processes and life patterns. It was difficult, but being around others on this same journey, I felt safe to try it. I was in a fog, but this time being loyal was an asset. I almost blindly followed them because I wasn't sure where I was going and how to get there myself. Even in the fog, I knew I was going somewhere I needed to go.

I was a finite thinker and I asked one of these dear saints how long it would take for me to "get there." She responded with something like, "There's no 'getting there,' the journey is the destination." I understand her now, but then, I didn't get it. "Certainly, she's wrong, there's always an ending."

Have you found yourself in this situation; you know you need to reevaluate, reconsider, or see things with new eyes? You are sure there is some sort of treasure waiting for you to take, but the journey is so unfamiliar.

I now needed to make a living. I loved being a stay-at-home wife and mother with some part-time jobs. Now, I had to ramp it up. Even though I had a business degree, it was 30 years old. If I'd tried to make it on my own, without the Lord, I wouldn't be where I am today. I had to surrender to him. It was hard and it was scary. The Lord gave me new eyes and a deeper understanding of what it means to rely on him.

There are times I long for the constant desperate dependence I had during those hard times. I know it should still be present but I, like many others when things get better, get caught up in the day-to-day routine. Hours will go by. Days will go by. When I stop and realize I've gone on through the day on my own power, I feel regret. God's power and direction is so much better than mine. When I remember this, I stop and pray, sing, and talk to him to get refocused on his day for me.

The Lord's work with me is not done. Is his work ever done? Not with me, anyway. I am a new creation, formed by him and by others who have been his hands and feet as I navigated and still navigate this truly incredible journey.

As I thought about what new career I wanted, I decided to become a motivational speaker for women. I wanted, as a speaker, to encourage others, no matter their story.

To be a reputable speaker, I believed I needed additional credentials. I went back to get a master's degree. By God's design, I ended up in a counseling program and became a Professional Counselor and a Marriage and Family Therapist. What a surprise. I never planned on being a therapist. Even though it delayed my dream of becoming a motivational speaker to large audiences, I now enjoy being a motivational speaker to smaller audiences – my clients.

I wrote this material as a Bible study called *REALLY LIVING*. I received the most comments on the *REAL* part of the study. It is practical and helpful for improving and fostering healthy relationships in all aspects of our lives. Later I expanded the title of my material to *REAL Influence*™, *A Foundation for Healthy Relationships*. *It's Me, Not You* is part of this material. In the future, I plan to write a book titled *Family Dynamics in Caregiving*, using the same components in REAL but with different applications.

It's Me, Not You provides practical and spiritual truths, and illustrations. Solutions are presented to reduce or eliminate barriers to healthy relating. We are often unaware some of our old habits or thought processes are problematic because they are habitual or cultural. *It's Me, Not You* names, describes and illustrates how they can harm relationships and inhibit a person's emotional and spiritual growth.

Introduction

We love having them and at the same time we hope some will go away. Some are wonderful, some are tough, and some we wish were never created. They are everywhere. They're in our home, at work, church, our neighborhoods, and our spiritual life. We even have some on our phones, podcasts, YouTube, blogs, radio, and television, or we feel like we do. What are they? They are relationships.

Relationships, relationships, relationships! They are the best thing ever and the most challenging thing ever. Because you chose to or someone suggested you read this book, it's likely you desire more meaningful, healthy, and enjoyable relationships.

Relationships are the cornerstone of our lives. Improving and refining them is something many of us understand and desire, but don't know how to do it or don't do it well. We'd like to know, but we still get tangled up in our own stuff or that of someone else.

All relationships are connected within us. If we are out of sync in one relationship, we are, likely, out of sync in other relationships. Most of us desire healthy relationships, but they elude us no matter how hard we try. There's no absolute magic formula, but I do know, readers who take this material to heart and make the changes needed, will have the foundational tools for healthy relating.

Organizations are also a community and have relationship problems. These problems can affect the bottom line and an employee's sense of well-being. When an organization supports an environment that encourages healthy relating and interacting, it increases individual and team productivity and profitability. *It's Me, Not You*, part of the REAL Influence™ series, provides an effective workshop for businesses that encourage healthy relating in the workplace.

Join me and learn the components that create healthy relationships, tools that prevent unhealthy relationships, the perspectives we need to have and the role our spirituality plays in developing and maintaining healthy relationships. This book does more than just teach *about* healthy relationships it's truly a tool kit providing the "how to."

Most, if not all, cultures around the world speak and write about relationships and community. Centuries ago, the Bible confirmed we are designed to be in relationships, in community. In Genesis 2:18, God pronounced "...It is not good for the man to be alone. I will make a helper suitable for him." He created Eve and then came community.

Being in community has a practical side. For centuries, survival was dependent on community for protection, food, and producing offspring. Most animal groups live in community for these same reasons. It just makes sense.

We are born in community, we thrive in community, and we rest in community. With good relationships, we have good community. With healthy relationships, we have healthy community. With unhealthy or dysfunctional relationships, we have an unhealthy or dysfunctional community.

Mahatma Gandhi, Indian lawyer, politician, social activist, and writer once declared, "The golden way is to be friends with the world and to regard the whole human family as one."[i] Jimmy Carter, former USA President, echoed the same theme when he said: "Each of us must rededicate ourselves to serving the common good. We are a community. Our individual fates are linked; our futures intertwined; and if we act in that knowledge and in that spirit together, as the Bible says: We can move mountains."[ii]

Theodore Roosevelt, another former USA president, also expressed a way to improve our relationships. He suggested: "The most important single ingredient in the formula of success is knowing how to get along with people."[iii]

When I was young, I don't remember questions or comments about healthy relationships. The only relationships I had to think about were not being mean to my younger sister and getting out of the way of my older brother and sister. I think it's safe to say back then, my family, and possibly society, was more task-oriented and less likely to question the health of relationships.

Today, we talk and read about the value of healthy relationships. We know they are important but the "how to" seems to escape us. Personally, and as a marriage and family therapist, I know the route to achieving healthy relationships has rough patches, blind spots, curves, and dead ends. "Will it ever smooth out?" we ask. Yes, but it takes work.

Several years ago, I had to examine and change some of my thought processes and life patterns. It was hard and then I came across this scripture.

> "I am the true vine, and my Father is the gardener. He cuts off every branch in me that doesn't produce fruit, and he prunes the branches that do bear fruit so they will produce even more" John 15:1-2.

This verse resonated with me but I wasn't sure I liked it. For plants, pruning produces healthier, more beautiful, and robust plants. I thought, "This is all well and good for plants, but it sounds too tough for me."

I went through a lot of pruning and still do today. I believe I'm healthier now and stronger because of the pruning and staying on the vine.

I admit, it can be difficult to stay on the vine, sometimes excruciating. I am grateful for the grace and mercy God extended and continues to extend to me during my difficult times. To become relationally healthy, some pruning has to take place.

Even though my profession as a therapist is to help heal relationships, I continue to work on myself and my relationships. Some are a joy to my soul and need little work. Others, well, I'm still working on them. This personal work is good but can be uncomfortable when I look at my own flaws. Who likes to do that?

The road of self-reflection and healthy relating is not without potholes. There are emotional and spiritual road blocks that weigh us down, divert our attention, keep us agitated, and give us permission for negative processing. They prevent us from achieving our goal - healthy relationships. These obstacles aren't new or revolutionary, I present them in a way that's easy to remember and put into practice.

I use the acronym REAL. It is a great word. REAL means authentic, genuine, true. The word real implies trust: Real hero. Real gold. Real good. The Real deal. If we use the word *real* with the word *relationships,* it implies our relationships are authentic, genuine, and true. So how do we accomplish this? How do we acquire authentic, genuine and true relationships?

The REAL Influence™ series provides a solid foundation for building healthy relationships with family, co-workers, and community. REAL Influence™ identifies and expands on the four obstacles that inhibit the development of healthy relationships. Solutions and tools are offered to help change our thought patterns and actions in order to create a positive influence. We will address Resentments, Expectations, Acceptance and Letting Go. I invite you to come along with me in living REAL, obtaining REAL freedom, and achieving REAL Influence™ in all your relationships.

Note: I use stories to help illustrate concepts and ideas. All stories are about me and my family or they are fictional created for an illustration or concept I'm addressing. None of the stories are my client's stories.

Chapter 1
It's Me, Not You

Before we hunker down to learn all we need to know about healthy relationships, I want to explain our responsibility in this process. We are in charge of the status and health of our relationships. It is up to us, not anyone else. We can be in relationship with people who are relationally unhealthy but still keep ourselves healthy.

This book is for you. If you bought it for someone else because you want them to change, it's not going to happen. I wrote this for you. You are important. Giving someone a book because you think they need to change doesn't work. It's about the change they see in you that matters. They need to see and experience a healthy difference in you. If they are curious about how you've changed, how settled you are, or how relationally healthy you are, and want to know "how" you did it then yes, give them this book.

Okay, let's get started. Each day we experience all kinds of relationship's ups and downs. We do great on some days and stumble on others. We get back up and try again or we hide and give up. If there is discord, we play a mental guessing game wondering who was at fault or if there was an "at fault." Yes, life is unpredictable. Some outcomes confuse us and we wonder what to do, then a perfect day shows up. *It's Me, Not You,* doesn't guarantee every day will be perfect, but it sure helps pave the way for more peaceful days when it involves our relationships.

1

On days when we experience friction, do we spend too much time figuring out who is responsible? Do we justify our words or actions so we aren't blamed, no matter the context or situation? I've experienced this confusing back and forth. I try to remind myself my thoughts are a matter of my perspective. It's all in my head and I tend to roll it around, sometimes day and night. I don't want it to be "my" fault. I think and rethink all the details so I can come up with a different outcome. I catch myself and tell myself to stop… "I don't need to get trapped here."

The health and strength of our relationships with God, family, friends, and associates is dependent on how we process situations and who we believe is responsible if there's conflict. Most of us don't want to be responsible for conflict or discord; we want to blame someone else. There's a problem here. If solving the conflict is someone else's responsibility, we can't move forward. We are waiting for a change, a repair, a different approach from someone we have no control over. We only have control over ourselves.

Taking the position, *It's Me, Not You*, keeps us in touch with reality and allows us to solve problems on our own. This position doesn't mean it's never someone else's responsibility; it means the power is within us, not someone else, to move us along. We don't need to wait for someone else to do or not do; say or not say, something. This can take years or it never happens.

There is so much freedom in the position *It's Me, Not You*. We can claim it, do what we can and then move on. It gives us REAL freedom and positions us to relate with REAL influence in all our relationships.

If you're feeling some resistance to this concept, ask yourself if you want or believe people need to be blamed, must pay, or you can't fathom letting them get away with something. As we explore the following chapters, we'll see, if we stay resistant, we have no movement. We gave the responsibility for our contentment to someone or something else.

The irony is, they're probably unaware of the responsibility we gave them. Second, if they are, they don't care or have enough retort to counter our reasoning. Third, if we want to blame or make sure someone doesn't get away with something, we are their prisoner, sometimes for a lifetime.

Our goal is to have freedom in our lives by letting go of things that snag us, bog us down, blinds and discourages us. Below are some universal truths, shared by many across the centuries and the world, spoken to encourage us then and now.

"Man must cease attributing his problems to his environment, and learn again to exercise his will – his personal responsibility"[iv]
-Albert Schweitzer, Physician, Theologian

"Why do you look at the speck of sawdust in your brother's eye and pay no attention to the plank in your own eye?"
-Matthew 7:3.

"The price of greatness is responsibility."[v]
-Winston Churchill, Prime Minister of England

"When you think everything is someone else's fault, you will suffer a lot. When you realize that everything springs only from yourself, you will learn both peace and joy."[vi]
-Dalai Lama, Spiritual leader

"You, therefore, have no excuse, you who pass judgment on someone else, for at whatever point you judge the other, you are condemning yourself, because you who pass judgment do the same things" -Romans 2:1.

"Men must necessarily be the active agents of their own well-being and well-doing...they themselves must in the very nature of things be their own best helpers"[vii]
-Samuel Smiles, Scottish author, government reformer

Freedom comes when we realize and embrace the idea that our contentment comes from what we think, say and do. It is not dependent on our circumstances or what someone else thinks, says, does or doesn't do.

Our ticket to experience healthy relationships is within us. We need to take care of our emotional, spiritual and physical self, and how we respond to day-to-day situations. Our sense of well-being is also affected by: our positive or negative thinking, accepting or rejecting our circumstances, living in the present or the past, laughing or scowling, or making others responsible for how we think or feel.

We know we have control over what we eat, whether we exercise, or get the right amount of sleep. We also have control over our emotional welfare. *It's Me, Not You* addresses many aspects of our relational dynamics and offers the reader solutions and hope for improving relational difficulties. This hope allows us to live freer, enjoy positive and healthy interactions and have the REAL Influence™ components in our lives and relationships.

Together, we'll explore the four common factors, if not addressed, cause difficulties in our relationships. The acronym REAL represents these components: **R**esentments, **E**xpectations, **A**cceptance and **L**etting Go. The goal is to help us identify these elements in our relationships, understand them and find solutions to minimize their negative impact on our lives. We'll become free to live a life without negativity and blame. Using the suggestions offered, will help us find patterns that need adjustment, concepts we haven't thought about, and tools to make the adjustments needed. The position *It's Me, Not You*, gives us the freedom to depend only on ourselves to make the changes needed. No one else has to do anything, be anything, or say anything. Isn't this great? We can facilitate our own changes and live a life enjoying strong and healthy relationships at home, work and in our community.

Ephesians 4

Ephesians 4[viii] is the scriptural support for my desire to help others repair, build and enjoy healthy relationships. Why? In the first three chapters of Ephesians the Apostle Paul reminds the new Christians how grateful he is for them, what gifts they have and what their responsibilities are. He also gave them instructions about behaviors and relationships he believed new Christians needed to know.

Paul compared the habits, beliefs, and ways of relating the new Christians had before coming to Christ. Then follows with the habits, ways of relating and beliefs he recommended they now embrace. Chapter 4 is a caring message of welcome and instruction.

In Ephesians 4:1, Paul calls himself a "prisoner of the Lord." He urges us to live "a life worthy of the calling we have received."

In verses 4:22-24 he tells us we need "to put away our old self" and "to put on our new self. You were taught, with regard to your former way of life, to put off your old self, which is being corrupted by its deceitful desires; to be made new in the attitude of your minds; and to put on the new self, created to in true righteousness and holiness."

These four verses inspired me the most. The visual of putting off and putting on is easy to picture and understand. I know, years ago, the Lord wanted me to put off my old self and put on the new self he had for me. This was not a one-time event in the past. It continues on today and every day. The rest of chapter 4 gives us more instructions about how to relate and live with each other in healthy ways.

Ephesians 4 contains the essential ingredients for healthy living. It supports my desire to help others repair, build and enjoy healthy relationships.

Other verses in chapter 4 explain how we should treat others and how we need to change certain behaviors within ourselves. This chapter has clear verses explaining what's expected of us as we grow into our new self.

The rest of chapter 4 is specific about the changes these new Christians needed to make and their new responsibilities. No matter your faith, Paul's instructions are good for us all. They are listed below with the verse in parenthesis:

1. "Live a life worthy of the calling you have received." (1)
2. "Be humble, gentle, patient, bearing with one another in love." (2)
3. "Keep the unity of the Spirit through the bond of peace." (3)
4. "Reach unity in faith and in the knowledge of the Son of God." (13)
5. "Receive your calling." (13)
6. "Do not be tossed back and forth by the waves, and blown here and there by every wind of teaching and by the cunning and craftiness of people in their deceitful scheming." (14)
7. "Speak truth in love." (15)
8. "No longer live as the Gentiles do, in the futility of their thinking." (17)
9. "Put off your old self and be made new in the attitude of your minds." (22)
10. "Put on your new self, created to be like God in true righteousness and holiness." (24)
11. "Put off falsehood and speak truthfully to your neighbor." (25)
12. "In your anger, do not sin. Don't let the sun go down while you are still angry." (26)
13. "Do not steal, work instead, share with those in need." (28)
14. "Do not let any unwholesome talk come out of your mouths, but only what is helpful for building others up." (29)
15. "Do not grieve the Holy Spirit of God." (30)

16. "Get rid of all bitterness, rage and anger, brawling and slander, along with every form of malice." (31)

17. "Be kind and compassionate to one another, forgiving each other". (31)

Wow! The Apostle Paul gave us good instructions for healthy relationships. All his teachings fit the heartfelt message I want to send in this book – *let's learn how to build and enjoy healthy relationships.*

Is it possible to have healthy relationships even if others don't follow our lead? Yes, we can still relate with integrity and without drama. We don't have to wait for anyone else to do or not do something. *It's Me, Not You.* What great news!

It's Me, Not You Reflections are in the Appendix.

Chapter 2
Resentments

Matt's view outside his office window is spectacular. Today, he had so much on his mind he was unable to enjoy the stunning sunset. He debated whether to call his sister about the thoughts he had suppressed for months. He wasn't sure about including her in the steps he wanted to take, but decided to find out.

"Hey, Andrea, can we meet for lunch this week?"

"Sure, what works for you? I can't do Wednesday or Thursday."

They met at their favorite restaurant a few days later. After some small talk, Andrea asked, "What do you want to talk about?"

"I've had it with Gene and Colleen, they're draining Mom and Dad."

"Really? Did they say something to you? I know Gene and Colleen haven't been pulling their share but Mom and Dad haven't said anything to me."

"Well, they haven't actually said anything to me, but it isn't right they're bumming off them. Colleen barely has a job; Gene isn't working and both have messed with drugs. Gene disappeared for two years! You and I made our own way in life but they aren't even close. It isn't fair and we should say something to mom and dad. It bothers me and I think about it a lot."

"I don't think about it much, but if you feel this strongly, I'll go with you. When do you want to meet with them?"

Matt and Andrea are on the edge of a slippery slope toward the pit of resentments. They feel justified in their position of trying to protect their parents from their younger siblings. They believe they see the situation clearer than their parents. They may not know they're inviting in one of the major destroyers of relationships – resentments.

Have you ever thought you see a solution clearer than someone else? If they didn't agree with your perspective, did you feel resentful toward them?

Resentments can damage relationships both horizontally (family, friends, co-workers) and vertically (spiritually). Matt and Andrea feel they are protecting their parents and trying to help mature their siblings. When a position feels justified, like this one, there's usually minimal awareness a resentment is being created. The feeling seems justified. This is understandable.

A similar scenario is found in the Bible. There's the story of the prodigal son. You can find it in Luke 15:11-32. The scene is: The younger brother left the family and took his inheritance and squandered it. The older brother stayed, was responsible and faithful to his father. After living in squalor, the younger brother returned home. Their father celebrated the younger brother's return with a great party. The older brother was resentful this wayward younger brother was welcomed back with a celebration. He felt justified, after all, he had been faithful, stayed with his father, did what his father wanted, and apparently never caused problems. The older brother was caught up in the fairness/justice issues and formed a strong resentment toward his brother and his father.

Resentments aren't good. We don't want them. They bog us down and keep us in negativity. They can lead to bitterness which is like concrete to the soul. They affect our relationships, our sleep, and cloud our thinking.

In this chapter, we'll explore what resentments are and where they come from. Chapter 3 will continue with why resentments are harmful, other choices we have, how to release them, and how to prevent them from forming. Come along with me as I offer a process to enjoy healthy relationships, obtain REAL freedom, and have REAL influence in all our relationships.

What is a Resentment?

"Resentment is like drinking poison and waiting for the other person to die."[viv]
-Saint Augustine, 4th century philosopher

If someone asked me 25 years ago whether I had a resentment, I would have answered a profound "no." A few years later, when I realized what a resentment is, I had to admit I had them. I started working on releasing them and continue to work on not creating any more…sometimes it can be hard to do. When I finally release them, I feel negativity and heaviness leave my body.

What do you think about resentments? Have you thought about them? Are you aware you have some? Are they a normal part of your life? If they are, are you okay with them or do you know they're not helpful, but don't know what to do with them?

Let's look at what a resentment is. They are usually strong negative feelings that come from a sense of being wronged or criticized. Resentments usually have some blame attached to a thought or feeling we have. They can come from an action or inaction of someone, something or some event. Resentments are full of negative energy and bog us down. They can severely damage relationships and prevent us from experiencing healthy relationships. Whoa…is this what we want?

Resentful feelings are also present in our perception of unfairness, unmet expectations, and misunderstandings. They can emerge when we feel jealous, fooled, betrayed, unappreciated, or taken advantage of. They also show up when we're taken by surprise or feel rejected. Once we allow resentments to form, we often justify these negative thoughts. Sometimes we welcome other resentments to join in. "Hey, come on over here, we're having a resentment party. Join us!"

I grew up on military bases which was great as a kid. Black and white thinking was common, probably necessary in the military. One of the results of this type of thinking was, in my mind, there was only one way to think and one way to do things. As a result, when I became an adult, I got irritated if things didn't go the way I thought they should go. Showing irritation was not encouraged so I let the negative feelings sit inside me. Because looking good was important, any negativity had to go down under. I never considered these feelings might be resentments. So, we get back to the question: Are we aware of our resentments? We may see resentments in others, but how about ourselves?

While watching the news, talk shows, and social media posts we see resentments flying all over the place. The entire plotline in many fiction books and movies are based on resentments and the consequences they bring, often murder. If the resentments were voiced as disappointments, instead, there might be more peace and problem solving available, but, instead, resentments bring out our anger.

The Bible has multiple examples of resentments. Cain was jealous and resented Able. Sarah was jealous and resented Hagar. Joseph's brothers were jealous and resented him. David's children resented each other. Jesus disappointed the Jews and they resented him. There are more examples of resentments in the Bible and nothing good came out of any of them unless God intervened.

Getting back to Matt and Andrea. Taking a deep breath, Matt pulled up to his parents' home. While they walked up the sidewalk, Andrea started to hesitate but followed her brother.

"Hey, Matt and Andrea, it's so good to see you, come on in," their mom hugged them as they came through the door.

Matt looked at his dad and said, "We need to talk, Mom and Dad."

"Well, sit down and tell us what's on your mind," smiled their dad.

His back rigid, Matt began, "It's time for you to tell Colleen and Gene you're not going to support them anymore and they have to leave your home."

"I agree," Andrea added sliding a little lower in her chair.

There was a pause, then dad responded, "Thanks for your concern, but we're fine with this arrangement."

Matt continued to try and reason with his parents and persuade them to see reality – Matt's reality. Andrea's voice was low when she chimed in. The meeting ended with Matt saying, "I'll have trouble coming over here. I can't stand watching them take advantage of you. You're enabling Colleen and Gene. They're not doing anything to help the two of you. We're just trying to show you how much we care."

Through her tears, their mother responded, "We can't beg you to come over, but this is our business, not yours. Your dad and I are okay with the situation."

As they left the house, Andrea asked Matt what he thought.

"They'll think about it and realize we're right."

"I am not sure, Matt. I am worried. Maybe this isn't our business."

The apostle, Peter, has some strong words about what happened with Matt and Andrea. In 1 Peter 4:15 he talks about suffering. "If you suffer, it should not be as a murderer or thief or any other kind of criminal, or even as a meddler."

The NLT version of the Bible replaces meddler with "prying into other people's affairs." The New King James Version (NKJV) replaces meddler with "a busybody in other people's matters." This is pretty strong stuff. Meddling in other people's business is in the same sentence as criminal activity. We need to sit up and take notice of this.

Plato[x] also has some advice for us - "Justice means minding one's own business and not meddling with other men's concerns."

By making their demands and not considering their parents' perspective, Matt and Andrea created a situation that isn't easy to rectify. It's common to feel like you're right in a situation like this one without realizing the relationship damage that might take place.

If their parents were truly being taken advantage of and were naïve, there is another solution. Call Adult Protective Services. This wasn't the case in this scenario.

Where Do Resentments Come From?

When I admitted I had resentments, I was convicted I needed to address them. As I worked on understanding them and why I formed them, I had an unexpected *ah ha* moment. My resentments come from me! I create them, I'm responsible for them. What? Is this even possible? I always thought another person or thing is responsible for my resentments because my resentments are about someone or something disappointing me or hurting me. I realized even if my resentment is about someone or something else, I still created it. I had other options. We will learn more about these options as we go along. Ann Landers[xi], in her newspaper advice column, gave us a great quote to remember about resentments. She said:

"Hanging onto a resentment is letting someone you despise live rent-free in your head." Yuck, I don't want that. The irony here is it is good news I'm responsible for my resentments. Why? If I'm responsible for creating them, I have the power to get rid of them. No one else needs to do anything. I don't have to wait for years for someone to do something or not do something. I created it so, I can get rid of it, right now, because I'm in charge of my own resentments.

It's still a struggle to own the fact I have resentments and I create them. I thought I wouldn't "look good" if anyone knew. For me, it feels much better to blame someone else for how I feel. I know this seems counter-intuitive, but many of us have a strong desire not to look bad or be wrong.

There are other choices than creating a resentment. I can be sad or disappointed. I can choose forgiveness or letting go. Before I create a resentment, I can choose to discuss my feelings with someone who knows and cares about me. Creating a resentment is a choice. The only one who can create and release my resentments is me. Darn, now I can't blame someone else.

Does this surprise you? Does it relieve you? Do you see the freedom it brings you? Or, do you disagree?

Anger and Resentments

Resentments are often a camouflaged form of anger. In the past, I believed I rarely became angry. As a general's daughter I wanted to look good and be good. Being angry doesn't fit the bill. Admitting being angry or having a resentment can be difficult. I considered myself as a person who extended grace and mercy so why would I ever be angry or resentful?

I created a smokescreen by using more acceptable words masking the fact I was angry and resentful. I would call my resentment something more acceptable like: *a difference of opinion or an annoyance.* Sometimes I would rationalize them by thinking *at least I pray for them or one day they will thank me,* or the worst one of all, *I know what's best for them.*

Once I admitted I had resentments it still seemed cleaner and less harmful than admitting anger. Being angry and resentful is not one and the same. Anger comes before resentment and is a primary gateway to resentments. Since it's only a gateway, we can pull back and not go forward.

Let's talk about resentments and concrete. Image our feelings mixing together in a concrete truck. We have sadness, disappointment, and betrayal turning and mixing. When it's time to pour the concrete mixture, all those feelings hit the air and result in each one hardening and turning into concrete. The more they hit the air, the more opportunity they have to harden. Now we have less opportunity to release them.

When the mixture is still wet, we have a chance the resentments won't set. Once we've allowed the feelings to turn into concrete and harden, we are stuck. We have to use a jackhammer to break them up.

Admitting anger is healthier than sitting in resentment. Admitting anger is honest and has more solutions available. It took someone I've known for almost 20 years to point out this truth to me.

I was in a difficult place. We had unexpected trials in several categories during a six-month period. My husband was laid off. There were serious problems with two grandchildren. We had two fires on the same day. One was at our house and put out quickly. The other was a storage facility. Our unit was incinerated and we lost many precious items.

I thought I was experiencing burnout. I had trouble sleeping and could tell I wasn't smiling as much. I was sad and felt tired all the time. Therapists must be aware of the possibility of burnout and take appropriate steps to solve it. I made an appointment with the therapist who helped me years before. After listening to me for about an hour, she challenged me to consider I wasn't sad and I wasn't in burnout. She suggested I was angry, very angry. I discounted her observations at first, after all, I didn't see myself as an angry person.

Because of my resistance, she asked me to tell her one thing I might be angry about. I started slowly, with some anger about our pets, then some anger about a family member. Before I caught my breath, I listed at least 10 things I was angry about, and some were huge. I was shocked but at the same time relieved. "Wow," I thought, "I can do this, I can reframe some of my situations and I can deal with this anger."

Besides being a primary ingredient in a resentment, unacknowledged anger can create depression, stress, and fatigue. Admitting my anger freed me. When I drove home, I felt so much lighter. What a relief! It's ironic that admitting my anger was a relief.

Assumptions and Resentments

Assumptions, like anger, are a gateway to resentments. Think about some assumptions you've made lately. How did they turn out? Were any problems solved? Sometimes our assumptions are accurate, but not often. Assumptions are thoughts, ideas, and beliefs we have, but without proof because we haven't consulted with anyone. Most of us make assumptions, sometimes without knowing it. What happens is we make assumptions and jump to conclusions before discovering the facts of the situation. Our conclusion becomes our reality and we operate out of this assumed reality without checking the facts with anyone.

People who jump to conclusions rarely land on solid ground. We jump to conclusions so we don't have to think about it anymore. If we're honest, we may like having a resentment based on assumptions. It means we don't have to do any work on our part to figure it out or work with another person. It's one and done.

When I didn't understand something someone said, did, or didn't do, I was prone to making an assumption. When I didn't understand a person's hurtful words or behavior, I often assumed it was about me or I caused their behavior. If someone didn't acknowledge me, I assumed I'd done something wrong. Many of my assumptions were unfounded. I just wanted to make sense of things and an assumption works, or so I thought.

When I make an assumption, I believe it helps me figure out the situation even if I'm wrong. Often, I start a debate in my head and over think things for hours. At some point, I stop and say, "Stop it. This ruminating is not good for me." Today, I recognize when I'm entering into the assumption world and I tell myself "don't step in."

Bob Newhart[xii] has a great YouTube video called "Stop It." Watch it and learn how to tell yourself "Stop it" if you find yourself overthinking about situations, things, people or events. Overthinking and ruminating are like fertilizer for resentments. But like fertilizer, they stink.

Assumptions created problems for Rob and Sheila. They started seeing a counselor to address communication issues in their marriage. After five sessions together, Sheila came in for an individual session and blurted out, "I can't do this anymore. I'm so lonely. Rob doesn't care about me at all."

Surprised by Sheila's intensity, the therapist asked a few more questions. Sitting on the edge of her chair, Sheila began to talk.

"When Rob comes home, he gives me and the children a kiss and then sits down and turns on the news. He doesn't ask what he can do to help. He never brings me flowers and when we go out to eat, we always go where he wants to go. I wonder if he knows or understands me." Leaning back, she reached for the tissues.

Rob and Sheila are in their thirties and have two young children. Rob has a job in a company he hopes will provide a good future. Sheila's job was in a growing industry and when the children came, she changed to part-time. Neither complained about their jobs or parenting the children. They did agree they weren't communicating well and were growing apart.

What Sheila was experiencing is common. Her concerns were not catastrophic, but they were building upon each another. It felt catastrophic to her. She allowed disappointments in Rob's behavior to turn into resentments. She believed Rob needed to change his behavior and this would be the solution to her distress.

When the two were together, the counselor encouraged Sheila to share what she said in her individual session, and she did. Stunned, Rob almost walked out.

"I feel blindsided."

After gathering himself, he voiced another perspective.

"Remember a couple of years ago when I came home, I was happy to see everyone. I gave you and the kids a kiss and asked if I could help. You told me 'no' in an irritated voice and then told me to sit down and watch TV until dinner was ready."

Rob never discussed this incident with Sheila until now. He decided it was best to stay out of her way when he came home from work.

"I admit I resented Sheila for being so cold to me, but what was the point of bringing it up? Sheila should know why I come home and don't help out, she set it up this way. I'm shocked she wanted me to bring her flowers; she never told me anything close to that. I'll ask her to please pick the restaurant when we go out, but she won't. I am tired of being the one to decide every time."

Leaning forward, she responded in a shaky voice.

"We've been married for 12 years and you should know I like flowers and where I like to eat. I'm being polite when I insist you pick the restaurant. I guess you don't know me if you don't know where I like to eat."

Arms crossed, she continued, "I have no idea what you're talking about. Of course, I need your help when you get home. I can't believe you would pick the television over me and the kids. Are you making this up?"

Both Rob and Sheila made assumptions about what the other one was thinking or feeling. Both were inaccurate. Over time their assumptions became facts in their minds and led to their resentments.

Have you made assumptions similar to this story? When couples come to my office and say they are having communication issues, it's usually because of assumptions, unrealistic expectations or a value system clash. We'll discuss this issue again in the *Evaluate Expectations* chapter.

"Yes" and "No" and Resentments

Resentments form when we feel compelled to say "yes" because if we say "no," we think we'll hurt or disappoint someone. We may believe the other person is disappointed in us, or thinks we're mean if we don't say "yes." When we say "yes" but want to say "no," we're not being true to ourselves. We're actually lying.

I spent years stuck in this trap. There is a name for it. It's called codependency. The guru of understanding codependency is Melody Beattie[xiii]. She's sold millions of her book *Codependent No More.* As a recovering codependent, I am grateful for her work. I can say "no" more than ever before. I can stop a conversation if I'm feeling shamed or manipulated. I don't feel responsible if someone doesn't step up. I don't need to fix others' problems. Guess what…I never fall into a black hole when I say no. This was a feeling I used to have. I am very much alive and living in REAL freedom!

The Bible addresses this same wisdom: "Simply, let your 'yes' be 'yes' and your 'no' be 'no,' anything beyond this comes from the evil one" Matthew 5:37.

Mahatma Gandhi[xiv] continues with: "A 'No' uttered from deepest conviction is better and greater than a 'Yes' merely uttered to please, or, what is worse, to avoid trouble."

My conclusion is: this truth has been around a long time. It behooves us to pay attention to the wisdom here. Saying "no" can be a healthy response and save heartache and frustration.

Let's look at a common situation found in places we volunteer: non-profits, schools, churches, businesses, and a variety of organizations.

Marcus approached Maria, "It's heavy on my heart, Maria, but we need to volunteer somewhere else. We're not getting the support we need here. We step in when others don't show up, we attend all the meetings. People can count on us, but I'm wearing out."

"I know what you're saying, I was afraid to bring it up to you. Our daughters should be number one. We're short-changing them. We seem to do everything because only a few ever volunteer to help."

Marcus moved toward the couch. "Sit down, honey, let's talk about this."

Maria leaned into him. "I'm tired."

"Me too. Do you think we should discuss this with Anna and Chris?"

Marcus called Chris and asked if they could meet with them. When they got together, he and Maria shared their weariness.

Chris spoke first. "It seems you two believe you are obligated to take responsibility for things you aren't responsible for. Anna and I did this for years. It created irritations and resentments. I hear the agitation in your voice because others don't step up and volunteer. Guys, this is your doing, not theirs. You don't need to take on a responsibility just because others aren't."

"Anna and I learned we can say no and not feel guilty. We used to say 'yes' whenever we were asked and then resented, we said 'yes.'"

Anna picked up where he left off. "Chris and I learned to let the void occur. If we didn't, we'd be too overwhelmed."

"What do you mean by letting the void occur, Anna? We're overwhelmed and wondering if we should volunteer somewhere else."

"That's not the answer. If you don't learn how to say no and set good boundaries for yourself, you will find the same problems anywhere. I suggest taking a class or reading about setting boundaries."

"That sounds kind of harsh and or even mean," Maria responded as she looked toward Chris and Marcus.

"I understand how you feel, but it's not. I used to feel the same way. All it did for me was create resentments and we don't want them. They wear you out and create a lot of negativity and victim thinking."

It never occurred to Marcus and Maria they were creating resentments and the resentments were taking their toll. They didn't know the value of saying "no" and not filling in when no one volunteers. Letting the void occur means we don't have to fill in when there's a need and no one else is stepping up. Many of us feel obligated to say "yes" or "I will" because of the incredible pull to say yes when we see no one else is.

We do this because we don't like the tension we're feeling if no one volunteers. It's about us; it's about our tension, it's not about those who choose not to volunteer. We need to ask ourselves if we were called to say "yes" or did we do it because *we thought we should.*

Don't make someone's responsibility your responsibility because you want relief from the tension you're feeling because no one is volunteering. Years ago, the tension and internal struggle to say "no" was too much for me. To gain emotional relief I'd say "yes" or "I will" and then immediately regret it and start blaming others for "putting me in this position." They didn't put me in any position; it was my own doing. We may want to blame our "yes" on someone else, but the truth is, we willingly said "yes." No one threatened some sort of torture to make us say "yes" or go along with something when we didn't want to. When I found myself in this dilemma, I'd often justify my decision to volunteer by convincing myself I could do it better anyway. Oh, what a trap!

When we say "yes" and find ourselves overwhelmed and resentful, we take on a martyr position. I thought martyrs were the ones killed in the Bible. I didn't know I was one inside because I was still living. A modern-day martyr is one who does more than they need to, then feels unappreciated and resentful. At times, we enjoy the martyr position in an unhealthy way. We like the accolades others give us for how responsible we are. This was me. As worn out as I was, I loved it when others saw how "sacrificial" I was. My friends who went down this road before me were observing my dance. I thought they were admiring me, but they weren't. They were glad it wasn't them.

If we do say "yes" in a situation we wanted to say "no," take responsibility for the "yes." We're not in prison; we have free will to say "yes" or "no." We can't have a resentment because we said "yes" when we didn't have to. Ephesians 4:25 tells us to "speak truthfully to each other." A must for healthy relationships.

It took me some time to understand this. I thought since I was capable and could do it, I should pick up someone else's slack.

If our friends say, "Wow, you have a lot on your plate," pay attention. We may think they're complimenting us but they aren't; they are thinking, "Are you crazy?"

Years ago, I was walking and chatting with a new friend. We shared the activities we were in and what our weeks were like. She responded the: "Wow, you have a lot on your plate." I wasn't wise enough at that point to understand what she said. At first, I took it as a compliment and then realized later she wasn't admiring me at all. She shared she was once like me but learned a better way to live. It took months to reprogram my brain to get it – I *can* say "no." Saying yes and filling the void was and is not healthy or responsible. I found out I will survive and so will others even if I say "no."

I thank this friend who walked alongside me during this time. Reprogramming is hard and takes time. She would take my calls and affirm me as the scales were coming off my eyes and my heart. I'm grateful for this friend, the 12-Step programs on codependency, and the support groups offered by Open Hearts Ministry in Grand Rapids, Michigan. I would not be the person I am today without them.

We've learned what resentments are and where they come from. Resentments inhibit our ability to have REAL relationships. The good news is we can do something about it. The next chapter continues our journey toward cultivating healthy relationships by releasing resentments. As we release our resentments, we're moving closer to living in REAL freedom with REAL influence in all our relationships.

Resentments Reflections are in the Appendix.

Chapter 3
Release Resentments

What was your reaction when you learned our resentments are our responsibility and no one else? Did you feel irritated, relief, anger, or *it's not fair*? Was it eye-opening or did you already know we're the only ones who can release our resentments?

A resentment is like a monkey on our back. We no longer need to feed it, but we are so used to it. Our monkey may even bring us comfort at times. Resentments can be a big part of our life and releasing them may feel like losing a supportive friend. The friend we believe we can give our negativity to and hold it for us.

Is anyone thinking, "Isn't there something that is someone else's responsibility in this gig?" Sure, we can go there, but giving someone else responsibility for our resentments is locking us up without a key to get out. So yes, we do have to do the work and this is good news. We're in charge of our own relational freedom. No one else has to do or not do anything, it's all dependent on us.

It is our choice whether we want to become relationally healthy and live in REAL freedom with REAL influence. It's our choice to experience emotional and spiritual growth, encouragement, hope, and peace. Sounds good to me. How about you?

We've learned how resentments are formed and that we have the choice and power to release them. Let's go a little further and explore how resentments impact us in all areas of our life: how are they harmful, how do we release them, and how can we prevent them from forming?

Why are Resentments Harmful?

Why are they harmful? Let's see what a relationship expert says:

"Our fatigue is often caused not by work, but by worry, frustration and resentment."[xv]
-Dale Carnegie, Author, Motivational Speaker

As we discussed in the prior chapter, resentments can eat at us from the inside out. They affect our health, our mood, and how we process things. They need to be looked at, acknowledged, and released. We know, resentments can turn into bitterness. Bitterness is like resentments to the 10th power. There are many quotes and scriptures warning us that nothing good ever comes out of bitterness. Let's see what they say.

"Never succumb to the temptation of bitterness."[xvi]
-Martin Luther King, Jr., Civil Rights Activist

"And do not grieve the Holy Spirit of God with whom you were sealed for the day of redemption. Get rid of all bitterness, rage and anger, brawling and slander, along with every form of malice" -Ephesians 4:30-31.

Were you aware how damaging resentments are? Besides bitterness, resentments create anxiety, depression, and health problems. They also shorten a person's life, lead to addictions, ruin relationships, and can be the reason for getting fired or being laid off. Resentments are heavy and weigh us down. They cause us to construct ruminations and negative mental discourses keeping us distracted during the day and up at night.

Resentments are like a disease, if not treated, they can ruin our lives. True, we can't always prevent diseases from attacking us; or we can't always prevent people, things, or events from attacking us. However, we can control how we respond to these attacks and whether to create a resentment or not. A resentment takes up a huge portion of our brain and soul. Even small resentments hang out in our head and we go over and over them in our mind. Bottom-line: resentments cause misery as depicted in this saga by an unknown author.

This is a great piece. Please read it slowly, every line is powerful. Hopefully, this will help you become more aware of the resentments you need to release.

Resent Somebody

The moment you start to resent a person, you become their slave...he controls your dreams, absorbs your digestion, robs you of your peace of mind and good will, and takes away the pleasure of your work.

He ruins your religion and nullifies your prayers. You cannot take a vacation without him going along. He destroys your freedom of mind and hounds you wherever you go.

There is no way to escape the person you resent...he is with you when you are awake....he invades your privacy when you sleep...he is close beside you when you eat, when you drive your car, and when you are on the job...

You can never have efficiency or happiness...he influences even the tone of your voice...he requires you to take medication for indigestion, headaches and loss of energy...He even steals your

last moment of consciousness before you go to sleep.
So... if you don't want to be a slave...let go of your resentments.

-Unknown[xvii]

Family and Resentments

Creating resentments can be habitual without realizing it. They can be part of a family's culture where it's normal to have and talk about resentments – like they are expected and perfectly acceptable. In some family systems resentments are considered a positive way of taking care of a problem. They're the topic of many family conversations. There's often a pride factor in having a resentment. If this family dynamic has been part of a person's life for years, identifying resentments as problematic may be more difficult.

We often withhold talking about certain topics with some family members, as well as some friends and co-workers. We want to avoid conflict. We process it as no big deal and it makes sense to us. The truth is, we're afraid we'll look bad, and might experience push back or lose the discussion. Unfortunately, this brings us more trouble and resentments because everything is still inside.

In the religious and political arenas, we may draw lines others aren't allowed to cross. We're resentful toward those who think differently than we do. Some family members don't speak to each other for years over these differences. Speak up, but if you don't speak up, it's on you. Don't create a resentment because you didn't speak up.

Keep Short Accounts

One key to avoiding resentments is to keep short accounts. Keeping short accounts means I don't let a lot of time pass before bringing up what's troubling or disappointing me. If I wait too long to bring up a concern, I often stash it away. Soon, another concern or disappointment appears. I don't address this either. Before too long, these disappointments and concerns build upon each other and develop into full blown resentments. Once they were annoyances but now, they're resentments. Choosing to keep short accounts can prevent resentments from forming. If too much time passes and we don't address it, we opened the door and invited bitterness to come in. Keep short accounts. Address annoyances or disappointments in a timely matter. If they aren't addressed, they turn into resentments. If they still aren't addressed, the next step is bitterness.

Don't *Should* on Anyone

Have you experienced disappointment from someone because you believe they "should have known?" As we learned in chapter 1, Rob and Sheila had a solid foundation for a successful marriage, however, they fell prey to making assumptions, not keeping short accounts, holding onto their disappointments, and entering the land of the *shoulds*. The land of the *shoulds* is when we hold another person responsible for knowing things and preferences about us, we haven't clearly expressed or explained. Our reasoning is: they *should* know.

When the *shoulds* show up, most communication ends with each person defending their position and pleading their case, instead of trying to problem solve with each other. Rob and Sheila both thought the other spouse *should* know what they expected. This created resentments in both because they didn't communicate their hurts and disappointments to each other. Creating resentments creates problems, not solutions.

This set-up is another example where couples say they're having communication issues. They are communicating, but without words. They are at a standstill. Many of us don't bring up things to our spouse, family members, friends, and co-workers because we want to avoid conflict. We'll process it as "no big deal." The truth is, we're afraid we'll look bad, make the situation worse, or lose the discussion. Unfortunately, it just brings more trouble and resentments.

Rob and Sheila decided not to talk to each other about their hurts and disappointments. Because they weren't open about their true feelings, they created a void in their marriage built on resentments and the *shoulds*. We'll discuss the *shoulds* again and secret contracts in the *Evaluate Expectations* chapter.

In our unhealthy thinking, we might believe forming a resentment is the higher road than confronting a situation because it appears to eliminate conflict. The truth is, it just postpones conflict and sets up the possibility of an explosion later on.

We may believe holding a resentment is an action on our part to solve a problem. It's not; it's the easy way out as it doesn't require any reconciliatory work on our part. Resentments can feel like we have the power, when in fact, it's quite the opposite. We've passed the power to someone else. We need to reduce the anger and resolve the problem as soon as possible. Therefore: "In your anger do not sin. Do not let the sun go down while you are still angry" Ephesians 4:26.

Choices Other Than Resentments

Are you feeling convicted you may need to pay more attention to resentments? Do you think you might have some? If so, are you wondering what to do about them? Join the club, I work on mine all the time. It seems like just as I take care of one resentment, another pops up because there's a new scenario. When situations or individuals create difficulties for us, we have other choices than forming a resentment.

It is best to be truthful to others and true to ourselves about how the person or situation is affecting us. Discovering the actual emotion is healthier. Are we angry, disappointed, or annoyed? Find good counsel, pray, and process the situation in a healthy way. Again, it is on us to be a part of solving the problem, not anyone else no matter how wrong we think they are. We are responsible for our own welfare. Ignoring the situation will eventually birth a resentment.

We can't always eliminate circumstances that produce a resentment, but we can choose how we'll react to them. If I'm at a point where a resentment starts showing its ugly head, I try to address it immediately. Sometimes I'll miss it because it seems minor, but that may be temporary. Resentments build quickly.

Some other choices available than creating a resentment are: (1) talk with a trusted friend, (2) forgive someone, (3) give someone grace or mercy, (4) accept the consequences of our own actions or inactions, (5) acknowledge our anger, disappointment, sadness, hurt or other emotion, (6) ask God and your support system to help you with this emotion, (7) focus on what is going right instead of what is going wrong, (8) settle an account.

Let's see how Jorge handled it.

"I can't believe this is a mess again," Jorge sighed as he entered the warehouse. Hearing the sigh, Ryan asked, "What's wrong?"

The warehouse manager was curious. Ryan respected Jorge. He was the best safety specialist the company had in years.

"I talk to the guys about how things should be placed safely, they agree, then a few days later it is back to the same situation as before. Even though you're the manager, I'm responsible for the safety of the employees."

"I'm with you on this one, it's frustrating and we're having an audit in two days."

"Well, it looks like it will be us again." Jorge responded with an edge in his voice. "Let's get to work."

Ryan agreed but added, "I feel like we're enabling these guys, and we probably are, but it will come back on us, not them."

On the drive home, Jorge went over the day. He and Ryan did a good job, even though it took two hours longer than they expected. Negative thoughts were flooding his mind. Jorge was close to creating resentments. "I wanted to get home earlier. Why can't they ever do what is expected? I wonder if Ryan could have prevented some of this. I am frustrated and angry."

Jorge remembered he had other choices than creating a resentment. He caught himself from reacting and decided to look at the positive side.

"Negativity will get me nothing but trouble. I got a lot of exercise. I was able to spend time with Ryan. The warehouse is back in order, and I don't have to worry if we'll pass the audit. There will be consequences for the men and better boundaries set for the future."

Jorge arrived home and was greeted by his wife, "How was your day, honey?"

"Kind of mixed but I got a lot of exercise, I was able to spend time with Ryan, and the warehouse is in great shape for the audit. How was your day?"

Like Jorge, when I admit I feel angry, disappointed or resentful, I free myself to look at other choices rather than allowing resentments to settle in and take hold. Jorge focused on the good in the situation instead of what went wrong. He didn't overlook and excuse but he didn't stay stuck in negativity.

Jorge's response was a healthy one. Even though he was disappointed, he didn't choose to be irritable when he got home. Jorge's response allowed him to gain REAL freedom and REAL influence at work and at home.

Do Resentments Protect Us?

I know it sounds odd we believe resentments can protect us. Does it make sense to you? Let me explain what I mean. I realized a few years ago I may use resentments to protect myself. Resentments? Protective? These words don't usually go together.

It makes sense to me now, knowing me. When I feel disappointed, afraid, sad, blindsided, or some other strong emotion, it's hard for me to recognize them as feelings I can take care of. The truth is, I can take care of those feelings more easily than I can a resentment. It hasn't always been the case. I used to run from those strong feelings. They are uncomfortable and I feel helpless. When I turn them into a resentment, I feel better, like I am back in control.

It used to be hard to talk to someone about the anger I felt toward them, so I gave the *appearance* of offering kindness instead. That seemed much easier. In reality, I was protecting myself, not them. Unfortunately, if I'm giving the appearance of, I'm burying it all with no solution, which is another way we create resentments. What a mess this resentment thing is.

I struggle the most with being blindsided, that's a big one for me. Recovering from feeling blindsided takes me a long time. My reaction can be so strong I don't realize I feel blindsided. I don't know what I think, but I know it's bad for me. When I'm able to settle down, I see clearly, I was panicking. A resentment feels much better than feeling blindsided or panicky. I am still working on this one and may for years to come.

In our Western culture, few of us are taught how to deal effectively with strong emotions. We're not taught how to discipline our emotions. We're not taught resiliency. We're encouraged through media, family, and friends to get out of what we call negative emotions: sadness, hurt, disappointed, afraid – and to get out of them fast. We do this by eating, exercising, spending money, and other non-productive strategies like creating resentments. You can probably name some others.

This doesn't work. Experience the emotion, don't stuff it. When we were raising our children, we wanted them to learn to calm themselves, so why don't we have this same expectation of ourselves, our older children, and other adults?

Creating a resentment seems easier and safer and I erroneously believed creating a resentment was protecting myself. It made sense that a resentment takes care of the uncomfortable feeling and it is now packaged up nicely. No one knows it's there, most of the time, not even me. Remember, I don't get angry...I'm back in control.

Our Emotions

Are you or have been afraid of your emotions? Do you down play their importance? Our emotions are some of our best assets. They tell us things. They send important messages to us. When I stay true to my emotions and not jump out of them choices are available to me in all kinds of circumstances. I can journal, read scripture, pray, talk with a friend, go for a walk. These are choices I know I have. When I'm resentful, I'm wedged in. Without getting help, there is little room for movement and staying there is a recipe for bitterness. I don't want that.

The Lord taught me he can handle my difficult emotions. He can help me get through them. Note: I said *through* them, not take them away from me. There's a huge difference here. It's a face it and stay the course position instead of run and bury it or become resentful position.

Several years ago, we had two of our adult sons living with us. At first things went well but later it began to wear on us. The boys did fine, but at some point my husband and I wanted them to move out.

We were going to church one day when I complained to my husband "I am tired of the boys living with us. I just want my life back." I was discouraged and worn out. Well, the sermon that day was taken from Matthew 16:25: "For whoever wants to save their life will lose it, but whoever loses their life for me will find it." I am not sure what the intended message was, but I know the message I received was: "If I 'want my life back' I will be losing the life I have right now. If I let go and live the life I have right now, I will be more content and God can work with me because this is my life, my reality." I was convicted and started accepting the life I had. A couple of months later, I started bargaining with God. "Okay, God, if I have to accept and live the life you've given me, then help me get *through* this."

This was significant, it was a turning point in my life. Now I ask the Lord to help me get *through* my troubles, not take them away because this IS my life. I do bargain with him now and then, but still trust the life I'm living is the life I am supposed to be living – there's no more "I want my life back."

Reflecting

If Matt and Andrea admitted they fell into the cesspool of resentments, they might have approached their parents differently by admitting anger and then offering problem solving rhetoric instead of demand. Matt and Andrea had no power to make the changes they wanted to see. It was their parent's responsibility, not theirs

Rob and Sheila realized their lack of clear communication with each other and making assumptions about each other almost ended their marriage. As disappointing as it was to find out neither one could read the other's mind, they knew they had to communicate what they were thinking and feeling to each other.

Jorge was quite successful in preventing resentments to enter in. He made up his mind to process his day in a positive way instead of a negative mode. He also didn't make assumptions or personalize the irresponsible behavior of the employees.

How Do We Release Resentments?

So, we've learned what resentments are and how they harm us. Now, let's look at how to release them. Visualize standing next to a cliff. There's a big sign warning us the cliff is near and to be careful. The sign says "Beware of Resentments." Many of us willingly pass by the sign, fall off the cliff, and land into the nasty pool of resentments. True to form we claim it wasn't our fault and we blame others. But we're still in the pit. The best plan of action is when we see the cliff and the sign, turn around and go in the opposite direction!

Practically speaking, do any resentments own you or are part of your identity? Do you believe releasing a resentment isn't fair because the other person never "paid" or is "getting away" with something? Remember, we are the only ones who can release our resentments. We're the only ones stuck with negativity. We need to free ourselves by releasing our resentments. It doesn't matter what someone else does or doesn't do. It doesn't matter whether they're repentant or not. It doesn't matter whether our life circumstances change or not. We are bound up if we don't release our resentments. The other person, thing or situation has even more power over us if we hold on and don't release them. Is that what we want?

Let's Do It

Do you have resentments you'd like to release? If yes, start with acknowledging them. The second step is to ask, "What's required of me to release it or them?" Does it mean someone would win who doesn't deserve to win? *Whatever game that is.* Would it mean I would have to give up my need to be right? *I'm not sure I want to give it up.* Would it mean I can no longer justify my victim or martyr thinking? *Which is addictive.* Would it mean I may need to forgive someone who is hard to forgive? *That can be hard to do.*

When we release a resentment, we are free to reflect on how much energy we spent on it and where this energy could be better spent. If we let resentments go into entitlement, we may end up with revenge. Revenge and bitterness are like twin siblings. And scary ones. When we release our resentments, poison leaves our bodies.

Many of us lump all resentments into one big ball of yuck and it seems too big to handle. A practical and effective way to release resentments is to separate all resentments and the different entities they belong to. First, determine how many people or entities you have resentments toward:

1. Get one sheet of paper for each person or entity. Put the name at the top of the page.

2. For each person or entity write on their sheet all the resentments you have toward them, large, medium and small.

3. Pray or meditate for resentments to be revealed to you.

4. Go to a trusted friend or family member and ask them what they have observed regarding any resentments they believe you might have.

5. Reflect on things you think too much about. There will be resentments there.

6. Be sure and list as many as you can, even the small ones, because those grow and invite other resentments to join in.

7. Take plenty of time to make the list.

8. Under each person or entity rewrite the list by putting the smallest or least important resentment first and the biggest or most important at the bottom of the page.

9. Make sure the list, if done on an electronic device, is transferred to a piece of paper. Visually seeing them on paper and then physically crossing them off the list is very therapeutic and personally impacting.

10. Look at the smallest ones. Are they still valid resentments? Are they resentments you still want to carry? Can you or will you cross them off the list?

11. For each remaining resentment ask yourself if there's something you could have done to prevent it from

forming. Is there a quote or Bible verse that's helpful for this situation?

12. Write the actual emotion next to the resentment. What can you do about the emotion today?

13. Address this actual emotion by journaling, talking with friends, praying about it, or seeking help in handling it.

14. Evaluate your resentments on each piece of paper. Decide what you can do to release them. Do you need to forgive someone? Do you need to have a conversation with someone? Do you need to accept there's nothing you can do about it? Do you need to forgive yourself? Do you just need to release it because it is taking up too much space in your brain and your emotions?

15. Ask for humility and wisdom and the "willingness" to release the resentment.

16. When you decide to release a particular resentment, document it somehow. Use a helium balloon to release it, write the resentment on a piece of paper and burn it, use your list to cross it off. Use different colors with personal meaning. Be creative, do what works best for you. Go on to the next resentment and follow the same procedure. Start crossing them off your list. You are moving along the path to REAL freedom with REAL influence.

You may be asking: *if resentments are so common and seem to be a normal part of my life, how do I prevent them?*

Preventing Resentments

Since we've learned what resentments are, where they come from, the harm they do, the choices we have and how to release them, let's look at preventing them.

How can we prevent a resentment from forming when we feel jealous, hurt, wronged, or betrayed? Acknowledge it's hard to do.

We scream out about how unfair it is or we're just minding our own business. We struggle with the unexpected or the disrespect. We never thought something would happen or what happened was just plain wrong. Just like a physical disease attacking us, we need to get help. Below are some suggestions on how to prevent resentments from showing up:

Talk with someone about what's causing the initial feeling.

Don't make assumptions.

Acknowledge the actual emotions: hurt, disappointed, neglected, sad, etc.

Resist the justification to hold on to negative emotions.

Address it with the appropriate person, if you can, and take ownership of your part.

Figure out what benefits you by creating and keeping the resentment.

Practice acceptance and letting go.

Don't take things personally.

Set boundaries.

Fix your part and move on.

Have reasonable expectations.

Let your yes be yes and your no be no.

Visualize resentments as handcuffs.

Apply the Apostle Paul's words in Philippians 4:8-9 to your life. We are to think about "Whatever is true, noble, right, pure, lovely, admirable, excellent, praiseworthy. Whatever you have learned or received or heard from me or seen in me put it into practice." Resentments don't fit this bill.

Our Next Step

Releasing our resentments is an important step in becoming relationally healthy and living in REAL freedom. Resentments create distractions. When they're present, the negativity interferes with our sense of peace, spirituality, mindfulness, and closeness to those we care about.

When we acknowledge the negative impact, resentments have in our life, we begin to free ourselves of this obstacle that prevents us from enjoying healthy relationships with everyone.

As we move on to the next chapter, we'll learn how evaluating our expectations influences and positively impacts us. We'll discover how evaluating them moves us further along to experiencing healthy relationships.

Release Resentments Reflections are in the Appendix.

Chapter 4
Expectations

Expectations can be wonderful. Watch the eyes and body movements of a young child anticipating something exciting they are about to do. Observe a groom's facial expression as his bride walks down the aisle. See the young wife waiting on the dock when her sailor's ship is coming in. Parents are happy, at the end of the day, when their family comes home. Planning a vacation creates the expectation of having a great time. Watching my children graduate filled a longing and expectation I had for them.

Expectations can be tricky. I've experienced expectations met and not met. I'm sure we all have experienced this. My expectations can get the best of me, which causes me to wonder if some are wrong or unrealistic. The answer is not an easy "yes" or "no." There are times expectations are simple and understandable, and there are times when they're confusing and problematic.

What are Expectations?

An expectation is a belief something positive or negative will or will not happen. It may be something we are looking forward to or worried about. Expectations are considered to be normal, probable, not probable, reasonable, or unreasonable.

Expectations are everywhere. We all have them. Do you have some right now? Are they creating a positive or worrisome response for you? Are you anticipating something wonderful will happen, or are you worrying about something else? We have expectations when we're hearing a joke, watching a TV show, going to a movie, going to dinner with friends, or can be the dinner itself. Expectations are in every part of our lives.

The nature of most expectations is we are hopeful or worried if our expectation will come true. We have expectations about family, friends, co-workers, neighbors, our faith, things, and events. People we know also have expectations of us. We have expectations for leaders of our country, state, town, and community. We have expectations of teachers, pastors, neighbors, as well as police, firefighters, and medical personnel. The most personal expectations are those of our family and friends. These expectations can create comfort, joy, disappointment, anger, or fear.

There are many public stories about expectations met and not met. The stories come from family, friends, co-workers, and the news. We hear about them every day. Some are uplifting and positive and some are disappointing or tragic.

The Bible has many stories of expectations. The Jews expected a different Messiah (Matthew 27:22). Martha expected Mary to help her out (Luke 10:38-40). Jonah expected God to use him differently (Jonah 1:1-3). The Israelites expected their trip to the Promise Land to be easier (Numbers 11:1-15).

My personal expectations create a sense of hope or concern something will occur according to how I believe it will or should occur. The "according to how I believe it will or should occur" is what creates potential problems. When I have an expectation, I have thoughts and ideas about how things will play out. I have good or troubled feelings depending on what the expectation is. I think about how I will feel, whether I will enjoy myself, or whether it will be a mess, or worse, trouble. The important question is whether my expectation is reasonable and healthy.

Where do Expectations Come From?

Expectations come from our experiences, culture, gender, family traditions, wealth, stage of life, personal values, passions, and many other things. This is normal. Some of our expectations require little thought. They are just part of our normal day to day routine. Some, we've thought a lot about. Some are about other people. Expectations can feel good, or they can be habitual or problematic. There are reasonable, unreasonable, acceptable, unacceptable, healthy, and unhealthy expectations.

Rob and Sheila were frequently disappointed with each other but didn't know why. They felt the other was failing them in some way. Their disappointments came from the expectations each had of the other, however, they didn't clearly communicate these expectations to each other. If they had, their relationship would be healthier and less contentious.

Think about the expectations you have. Have you clearly communicated them to the appropriate person or do you feel they "should know?" Don't get lost in the "they should know." In healthy relationships, we clearly communicate our expectations, even if we believe they should know.

Life would be simpler if we all understood the expectations of those close to us. One of the most common causes of conflict in relationships comes from unmet expectations. There's a simple reason for the this – the expectation was never clearly communicated and received. Rob and Sheila called their lack of understanding each other's expectations a "communication" problem. It wasn't a problem in communication, it was a lack of communication. Their expectations were not clearly communicated to each other.

The expectations I have about others are more about me and what I want or don't want. This is typical. We want things to happen a certain way, so we develop an expectation. Sometimes there's a happy ending. Other times there's disappointment. I expected someone to think or do something a certain way, but they didn't. I expected something to happen a certain way, but it didn't. I expected someone to be there for me, but they weren't. I become confused, disappointed, and perhaps angry.

When my expectations are met, I feel good. When they aren't met, I feel sad and disappointed. I expect to feel great, but I feel crummy. I expect to be in a different place in life, but I'm not. I expect family and friends to remember things about me, but they don't. I expect to get a certain job, but they gave it to someone else. Unmet expectations are hard and can involve God, ourselves, our family, our friends, things, and events.

It's important to acknowledge these unmet expectations. Why? If they aren't acknowledged, they can lead to resentments. To prevent this, ask ourselves if our expectations are reasonable, realistic, and plainly communicated. If it's a "yes," great. If it's a "no," then ask trusted family and friends to help you rework the expectation.

Note: The expectations I am talking about are the ones we consider normal for our general society. When these expected social norms are not met, professional help is recommended.

Dan worked for the same company and lived in the same town for twenty years. He had an opportunity for a promotion, but it included a move to a different district within the same company. Since the children were grown and out of the house, Dan and his wife, Emily, decided to take the promotion and the subsequent move.

"I am excited about taking this job. A move to another city might be interesting."

"It sounds like a great opportunity, Dan, and I think it will be fun to have a change. I think the kids will enjoy visiting us in a new place."

The first two months on the job were uneventful. Dan was learning the ropes in this location and getting to know his new co-workers. As the days became more routine Dan found himself feeling unsettled and discontented. He ignored it for a while and then brought it up to Emily one evening at dinner.

As he put down the menu, Dan's voice was intense, "This job isn't what I expected it to be. I'm struggling. I don't want to feel disappointed, but I do. Actually, it is not the job, it is my co-workers."

Emily leaned across the table, "I thought something was going on, Dan, you just haven't been the same in the last few weeks. What's wrong with your co-workers?"

"There isn't anything wrong with them as people. They just don't do the things I believe are important in a work environment. No one stops by my desk to see how my day is going, they don't share information on projects, and no one organizes lunches. It's so different. Everyone seems to be independent of each other, maybe even stand-offish. I am not sure who I am upset with, the people or the company."

They decided to enjoy their dinner and finish the conversation when they returned home. Later, Emily encouraged Dan to verbalize his expectations of the new location. As Dan explained them, it became apparent the culture between the two locations was quite different.

"Except for our product, it doesn't feel like I work for the same company. It would be better if it was more like the other location. There would be less employee dissatisfaction and better flow of information between employees. They should know this isn't the way to operate a productive business. Honey, I'm tired of talking about it, let's call it a night."

As they talked over the course of several weeks, Dan began to see his expectations weren't wrong. They just weren't realistic for this location. The things he loved about his old job weren't present in the new job. His disappointments were valid.

One evening Dan sat in their living room with his head in his hands. Emily walked in and asked him what was going on.

"I actually feel somewhat blindsided and betrayed. I know this isn't intentional but I am not happy with this transfer."

Emily walked over and gave him a tender hug.

"I don't know what to say, Dan, except I feel sad for you. Is there anything that's going okay with this job? Is there anything you do enjoy?"

Problems Expectations Create

I can easily fall into the trap of creating expectations of others I feel are necessary for me to feel happy or content. Now my sense of well-being is dependent on something or someone else instead of myself or my faith. When I base how I feel on what someone else is going to do or not do, who someone is or not, or whether something is going to happen or not, I've set my own trap for disappointment and I'm at risk for creating a resentment.

If things aren't going according to my expectations, I may press my point harder so others see my perception or expectation is the most reasonable. Sometimes my brain or emotions can't imagine the other person's view as better than mine or even valid. I need to watch out for this dynamic. I may then go into demanding and controlling behavior, something I don't like to do. It does slip in every now and then without me realizing it. This is a common situation, especially in family dynamics.

If I don't catch myself, I may go down the path of working hard to convince others to see it my way. I'll restate my position or idea. If that doesn't work, I'll say it another way or bring up the past to establish my view. Later, I regret not taking the time to understand another's expectation or perspective. I was on a roll and didn't see I was disrespectful.

Many of us get caught in this trap and don't realize it for several hours or days. The conclusion is, don't create expectations others haven't agreed to. If they did agree and didn't follow through, then ask if you can step in.

Does this resonate with you? If so, take heart and keep working on it. The goal is to live in REAL freedom and have REAL influence in our relationships by healthy, not demanding relating.

Family and Expectations

What is your reaction to this subtitle? This may be an area of your most frustrating and painful experiences. Family is hard and wonderful, painful and healing, dull and adventurous, and many other combinations. Sometimes our worst relating skills show up in family. We don't want it to, but it does happen.

As parents, we can force expectations on our children we assume are best for them but go against our child's vision of themselves. We try to influence how the family group should do things, because we believe our ideas and beliefs are the better ones.

As a family member, we can inadvertently shame other family members by discounting or dismissing their opinions. Family members often have expectations of other family members that haven't been agreed upon or aren't known. Yet, the disappointment is still voiced. We can respond that we are unaware of their expectation, but that might not take care of it. We need to ask for clarification. We don't need to go into guilt and shame even if our family members want us to go there. Family members are famous for shaming each other.

Members of the same family can be unaware there are several ways of viewing a situation. Because we are *family*, we may assume other family members see things the way we do. It's hard to accept they may view things differently. "We are family, we should be thinking the same about this!" We reason, since our view makes total sense to us and our perceived outcome is good, of course, others should think this way!

It is not guaranteed we will have the same expectations as our friends, family, and co-workers. We often assume we're on the same page and are surprised when they voice a different view or solution than ours. If my brain doesn't have the "receive" button turned on, what they say may not make any sense to me and I may not make any sense to them. This is another door for resentments to come in.

Some common differences we have regarding expectations are: planning or not planning what the family is going to do on days off, responsibilities around the house, which family to spend the next holiday with and the traditions involved, how often we call or visit extended family, how to raise children, and where to take the next vacation.

It's important to remember just as we have trouble seeing or understanding another person's expectation or point of view, they also have trouble understanding our expectation or point of view. It doesn't matter how right we think we are, others may not see it the way we do. In the larger scheme of things, both can work. Acknowledge the differences and then problem solve. This is the best solution.

Assumptions and Expectations

There are days when I feel emotionally out of sorts. As the day goes on, the feeling doesn't go away. When I'm expecting something that doesn't materialize, I try to figure out "why" it didn't happen. I want to make sense of it all and have a reason for my disappointments. I'll make assumptions not based on facts. The made-up reason is usually a negative one.

"Why haven't they returned my call? Are they mad at me?"

"Why didn't they check on me. Don't they care?"

"Why didn't they ask me about it first? I have experience."

"Why didn't they pick up the slack? I guess they didn't want to be involved after all."

I used to be good at this, but what good did it do me except temporarily settle me down? I've worked on this for years and now recognize and eliminate these patterns quickly. If I give it the time, I find the reason is something else. It's not negative at all, and not about me. I eventually see my frustration and annoyance is because I assumed the "why" it happened or didn't happen.

I ask myself, "How did I get here, what path did I take?" I did it again. I made an assumption without checking it out. No wonder I feel out of sorts, I wanted things to turn out the way I wanted them to.

There are times when we make the assumption that others think and feel like we do. How I see things and how I expect things to go may be different from the existing reality or may be different from how others see the situation. I'm surprised and can be annoyed when I realize they're not thinking like me. I have to be careful with this dynamic and not take things personally or become controlling.

There are multiple ways to view a situation or the actions of other people. It's important to realize my reality is *my* reality, your reality is *your* reality, their reality is *their* reality. The different realities can be just as valid as mine. I'm not aware another reality exists until the different realities crash into each other. This happens to most of us at one time or another. It's not because we're stubborn or unreasonable, it's because our brain or emotions processed the situation in a certain way and created the perspective and expectations we have and they have. There can be different realities for the same situation.

Accepting differing expectations and perspectives is one of the strongest elements in healthy relationships. We'll explore more in the *Acceptance* chapters.

Perspectives and Expectations

Anthony, Maurice, and Clint were walking down a sidewalk near their office as they were returning from lunch. A car on the other side of the road suddenly hit another car. Some of the passengers were hurt, but it didn't appear anyone was seriously hurt. The three called their employer and told her they witnessed an accident and would be late. The police arrived and eventually came over to take the men's statements. The three saw the same accident but each report was slightly different from the others. After the reports were made, the men continued to walk back to work.

Maurice crossed his arms, "Hey, man, why did you tell the cop the red car was speeding? It wasn't."

"It looked like it to me," Clint explained. "The accident wouldn't have happened if he hadn't been speeding."

"Naw, that's not right. The traffic light was changing and he ran the light, he wasn't speeding," Anthony added as he hit Clint across the back of the head.

"Watch it, man, I am not in a good mood. I don't even want to go back to work."

"The other driver was on his cell phone, and that's the problem," Maurice added. "He was a distracted driver."

The three friends continued to discuss their perspective about how the accident happened and who was at fault. Since each had a different take on what happened, they were still arguing when they got back to work. By the end of the day, they had many of their co-workers taking sides about who had the most accurate version of events. Did they ever consider it was a good thing there were different perspectives about what happened?

One of the most freeing things in life is to relate with others by understanding each other's perspective. We don't have to agree with them but can acknowledge how they see things. It's important to consider another's perspective when we form our expectations. It's respectful to look at the perspective we are coming from and the perspective they are coming from. Our spouses and our friends have different perspectives in many areas. Accepting differing perspectives makes life interesting and allows us to relate in a healthy way whether at work, home, or in our community.

This concept can be hard and a surprising wake-up call. Guess what? Others don't feel the same way we do. Differing perspectives can cause conflict. If we take a stand or have a definitive position on certain subjects, we need to realize others might see things differently. If we don't, arguments and division are more likely to occur. If we listen to or consider someone else's perspective, there is less discord. This is another solution for "communication" problems.

Unfortunately, most of us enjoy being right or believe our perspective is the one and only correct perspective. We fail to consider others see situations differently than we do. There's wisdom in James 1:19. He was very astute when he said, "Be quick to listen, slow to speak, and slow to become angry."

"Quick to listen and slow to speak" is one of the keys to healthy relationships and solving communication problems. I used to be calculating my answer in a conversation while the other person was still speaking. I was not quick to listen. I wanted to be quick to speak back. It is so disrespectful when we only half listen because we are trying to be quick to speak back. Try to listen well so we are equipped to consider what others are saying and understand their point of view.

It's important to respect another's perspective, especially if we don't agree or align with it. When we focus on being right or having the right facts instead of considering other points of view, more division occurs and resentful thoughts develop.

There are times we do acknowledge someone has a different perspective, but we're still tempted to believe our perspective is the right one or, at least, the better one. The healthy position is to accept another's perspective just for what it is, another perspective, without adding judgment to it.

Values and Expectations

Our perceptions, values, and expectations are connected. Differences are normal and expected. It's our reaction to the differences that cause the dilemmas. Arguments are unnecessarily created when there is a value systems clash. Discussions become personal and create a needless competition. Dialogue becomes defensive and stalemated because someone has to be right. If it's coming from our perspective, our values, then it's right for us, but not necessarily right for the other person. Each person is defending his or her position, and problem solving is not happening. If one person gives in or the subject is tabled and avoided for a while, we may feel like we're not heard or valued. As author Brandon Sanderson[xviii] explains, "Expectations are like fine pottery. The harder you hold them the more likely they are to crack."

It's healthy to have different values. It's healthy to respect others' values. It's healthy to acknowledge the different perspectives and problem solve the differences, a key solution to communication issues. It's important to identify and acknowledge a value system clash before the emotions get too high.

Doug and Jan were married several years before their first child was born. Their newborn daughter was two weeks old and very fussy. Mom and dad were tired but wanted to go for a drive. They decided to go to their favorite lake about forty-five minutes away. They thought the drive and change of scenery would lift their spirits. When they arrived at the entrance to the lake there was a shack that wasn't there before. They pulled up and discovered there was now a twenty-dollar entrance fee to the lake. They were surprised. Doug turned the car around and headed home as he said, "Well, we can't do the lake today."

Jan reacted, "Yes, we can. We came here to make a memory. Let's just pay the entrance fee."

Doug kept driving, "Jan, we just went over our budget last night and we didn't factor in the twenty dollars."

Turning around to look at their daughter, Jan continued, "But we wanted to take pictures here. She is our first baby."

They drove home trying to convince the other who was right and who was wrong. Several days later they were still divided.

Cynthia, a good friend, arrived a few days later to see the baby. When the baby was taking a nap, Jan brought up the situation at the lake.

"You know, I might be able to help. I recently listened to a podcast about value system clashes, and what you are describing may fit. It seems like Doug's value was to stick to the budget and your value was to make a memory. Jan, is it wrong to want to make a memory or is it wrong to stick to the budget?"

Jan took a sip of tea, "No, both things are good."

When we react intensely to a difference of opinion it's often because we believe our value system is being challenged or dismissed. Any time we personalize a perceived challenge, we frequently respond defensively. We consider the challenge as challenging who we are.

This type of exchange is also described as "communication problems." The communication problem in this story is each parent came from a different perspective or a different value system. Both perspectives had equal value, but they, unintentionally, tried to diminish the other's point of view.

Doug and Jan's story is an example of a simple value systems clash that went too far. They both had an expectation of how the outing would go. There was a minimal attempt to understand and validate the other person's expectation when the unexpected happened. The only reason this was called a "communication problem" is because they couldn't agree or see the other's perspective. They were communicating, but from different value systems. Talking from a different value system is not necessarily a "communication" problem, it's a "lack of understanding where the other person is coming from" problem.

Both clearly heard each other, but they had a hard time receiving what the other was saying because it didn't translate well into their differing perspective or value system.

Our spouses, family members, and friends can have differing values. We have some values we agree on, and that's why we feel close. There are others whose values are very different. It's not likely our values match up one hundred percent with anyone. The difference in values can be major or minor. It's usually the minor ones that cause the arguments, the arguments we rarely remember and started over something small.

Values That Surprisingly Cause Problems

Do we wear shoes in the house?

Do we take a loan or do we pay cash?

Who do we visit during the holidays?

Do we visit family or stay home on Sunday?

Do we wash clothes every day and fold them immediately?

Do we pay bills when they come in or on the due date?

Do we let our children be involved in more than one sport or activity?

And many more common everyday situations or tasks.

These are personal values and they're all acceptable. What's one you have that someone else struggles with? Each person might argue intensely because the argument isn't about the facts, but about each person defending their values and traditions. It makes total sense to one but is insignificant to the other. There can be constant strife when those close to us value something we don't or we value something they don't. We need to be cognizant of these differences and decide to problem solve instead of trying to prove one view is more viable than the other. Our values affect us more than most of us realize.

Let's move on and learn how to evaluate our expectations and the peace and freedom it gives us.

Expectations Reflections are in the Appendix.

Chapter 5
Evaluate Expectations

Since most of our expectations come from our values and perspectives, it's understandable how differences occur between people. We put a huge amount of energy into our value system and so do they.

"A" Way and "The" Way

Our values and perspectives often become "the" way of doing things instead of "a" way of doing things, and we believe those around us ought to follow suit. We have a hard time understanding their perspective, and they have a hard time understanding ours.

Making the bed when you first get up is "the" way for some but "a" way for others. A certain belief or value may be "the" way for us, but it may be "a" way for someone else. Refueling the car at a quarter tank is "a" way for some but "the" way for others. Arriving on time is "the" way for some and "a" way for others. I know I have as many "the" ways of doing things that are another person's "a" way to do things. I like to believe my way is "the" way, but there are very few "the" ways and hundreds, if not thousands of, "a" ways in this world. When the traffic light is red, "the" way is to stop the car. And I do!

Understanding this dance takes the personal side out of the differences. The arguments are less threatening, and problem solving is available. Jan and Doug didn't realize their value or perspective was "a" way of doing things not "the" way. Jan was coming from the North Pole and Doug was coming from the South Pole. No wonder they saw things differently.

Where do our "the" ways come from? They usually come from personal experiences and expectations that worked for us in the past, our parent's teachings, other teachings, societal norms, our peer experience, or just from our personal preferences. They can be pretty good stuff. Its just others may not see it the same way, and that's okay.

I struggle with people not letting me know they're going to be late. It's one of my values and came from how I was raised. If you're going to be late, call me. I now understand "late" is defined differently for each of us. Also, some believe the need to call if they are late isn't a priority. They are more relaxed about time, another value, which can be a good one in certain circumstances.

The simple concept here is, guess what, the other person doesn't share the same value(s) I do. They don't mind being late. They don't care about when or how to fold the laundry. They love things I don't care about. Doesn't this make the "world go around?" Isn't this what makes life interesting? Expectations are something we create about people, things, and events. We want a particular outcome. If our expectation isn't met, ask two questions: Was the expectation realistic or was it a want? Was the expectation clearly communicated or was there an assumption they should know?

Evaluating Our Expectations

The good news is we can evaluate our expectations. When we evaluate our expectations, we stay open to changes within the expectations instead of moving into a demand that our expectation be met the way we see it. Evaluating our expectations helps us discern whether our expectations of others and ourselves are reasonable and healthy. It also helps us discern whether the expectations others have of us are reasonable and healthy. This is certainly good news!

Even if my expectations are reasonable and healthy, how I communicate them can be a problem. I may use a tone or certain words that put the other person on the defensive. I may be communicating from an internal demand or expectation I believe this person should know or should have known. When we believe our expectations should be known by others but aren't, it's a signal for us to stop and evaluate why the communication is becoming difficult.

I have expectations I look forward to. I have normal everyday expectations of myself and others. I've learned if my expectation doesn't materialize like I hoped, I don't need to go into negative thinking. My faith, my family, and friends help me by confirming my expectations as reasonable and healthy or help me rethink them if they're not. The purpose of evaluating expectations is to reduce possible misunderstandings, accusations, resentments, and other negative reactions. Most of us want to get along with others, and managing our expectations is one piece in accomplishing this!

Our expectations can create problems in our relationships. Again, we frame it as "We're having communication issues," but it's really expectations issues.

We believe we know the way people *should* react in certain circumstances, and if they don't, we're hurt or believe we weren't heard. This confuses the other person. They don't know how to respond. In ordinary circumstances, when we believe an action or inaction is intentional, there's a slim chance we're right. Most people want to improve their significant relationships. If this type of negative processing happens too often, others may believe they never do it right. So, they just give up.

Healthy Expectations

Healthy expectations are communicated clearly and are clearly received. They're based on the reality of the situation, the reception of the expectation, and the agreement to the expectation. These expectations come from what we want to see happen or from the idea it will be for the common good.

A healthy expectation is one that can be modified if others involved want to modify it or if reality indicates the expectation is not reasonable. Healthy expectations don't have a hidden agenda and can be freely discussed and changed without criticism or judgment. These consider others' perspectives and values. If there are differing views and differing solutions, expectations can be negotiated.

Dan originally had normal, healthy expectations about his new job. As things developed and his expectations were not fulfilled, they shifted to resentments. The only person he talked to was Emily. He didn't bring his concerns to his manager. He found himself resisting the reality of his new environment instead of accepting his reality and then making the personal changes he needed to make.

Emily was wise in asking Dan if there were any positive things about his job. Resentments can cloud any good that's present. Thinking about what is going right instead of what is going wrong is good for our health, our sleep, our disposition, our family, our friends, and our spiritual life. Winston Churchill has some wise advice about this.

"The pessimist sees the difficulty in every opportunity; the optimist sees the opportunity in every difficulty."[xviv]

-Winston Churchill, former Prime Minister of England

The *Shoulds* and Expectations

In the "Releasing Resentments" chapter, we saw how easily we enter into the land of the *shoulds* and how these *shoulds* contribute to our resentments. The *shoulds* are also linked to our expectations. Some common expectations are: "People close to me should know what I need. I shouldn't have to tell them," "They should know when I am joking," "They should know we can't be late," "They should know better. I didn't raise him or her this way."

As we saw with Rob and Sheila, the *shoulds* are present in our close relationships. "He should know I wanted to go out tonight. I shouldn't have to tell him." "She should know I don't care about car maintenance." "They should know mom and dad need them to visit more often." "She should have offered because she knew I had such a bad day." "He should know I like him to kiss me when he gets home." "She should know I have to have at least half an hour to wind down when I get home." "You should know I'm grouchy in the morning."

The *shoulds* are also present in the workplace. "They should know I like the coffee pot ready by 8:00 a.m." "You should know when I tell you I am taking care of it, I am taking care of it." "You should know when the paper in the copier is at half full, paper needs to be added." "You should know the manager is not interested in these problems." "You should know the board doesn't want to be approached about this."

Sometimes the *shoulds* can create what some call "secret contracts." Secret contracts are when we create an expectation of someone, but we don't tell them about it because they should know; we shouldn't have to tell them. Yet, we still hold them responsible for knowing our expectation. When this shows up in my life, I ask them to see the contract I signed agreeing to the expectation presented to me. It gets a laugh, but the point is made.

All this can be pretty crazy-making stuff. We need to be careful that we don't *should* on anyone - our spouses, friends, children, co-workers, and ourselves. The *shoulds* can go on and on. Healthy relationships don't include the *shoulds* because healthy relationships clearly communicate their expectations and verify, they were clearly received.

Problem Solving and Expectations

Problem solving is the answer to many situations where there are differences in perspectives and values. These situations also include the *shoulds*. When we operate out of our perspective and values, our emotions can run higher and defending our position becomes too important. We don't understand others also have values that are equally valid. The following scenario is common in all kinds of relationships.

Anthony and Trever are roommates. Anthony likes a neat and clean apartment. Trever doesn't care one way or the other.

"Trever, I've tried to be patient about this, but when you put the cans away in the pantry, you put them in haphazardly. The labels should all be facing outward."

"Anthony, that's ridiculous!"

"No, it isn't. No one I know mixes the cans up like this."

"It doesn't matter to me and really, this is kind of stupid to be concerned about how the cans are facing. No one I know does it your way."

Anthony was furious and left the apartment. He didn't return until later and didn't speak to Trever for several days. Trever just shook his head in disbelief, "How dumb," he thought.

When we acknowledge someone is coming from a different way of thinking, we can problem solve the differences instead of becoming defensive or establishing our way as "the" way. Defensiveness is only a tool to establish ourselves as right. When these responses appear, it's best to end the conversation. This is another example that gets categorized as "communication issues." This is actually a perspective or values issue.

If a participant, in an argument, decides he wants to end the tension, they often give in. If this isn't done honestly, a resentment can develop. Giving in ends the tension in the moment but creates long term tension in the form of a resentment. If there are too many "giving in" situations, a martyr or victim position often shows up. The door is now wide open for resentments to turn into bitterness.

Problem solving is successful when one or more participants calls a halt to the conversation and acknowledges an impasse is happening. Each person takes his or her turn to explain their perspectives and values in the situation. The others must not judge, but instead listen to understand where the person is coming from. We've all heard the term "agree to disagree." This is part of the problem-solving solution as well as negotiation and compromise.

"Anthony, I won't be offended if you fix the cans the way you want them. I am sorry, but it's just not important to me, and I would get annoyed if you hold me to this task."

"It's hard for me to accept you don't see the value in this, but since it's more important to me, I'll fix them the way I want. I'll take care of it."

Healthy relationships experience acceptance of others' differences in values and perspectives. If we consider another's point of view as valid for them, we stay in problem solving. If we keep believing someone is right and someone is wrong, we're at a dead-end. We complain to others, we think about never talking to our family, friends, or co-workers again, we think about divorce, or we think about leaving certain friends. We go down this road because we are frustrated and don't know there is another road we can go down. The other road is acknowledging a values difference, accepting the difference, going into problem solving, and calmly talking about how to resolve the differences in both values and perspectives.

If, as they were leaving the lake, Doug or Jan acknowledged they were having a perspective or a values system clash, perhaps Doug could have pulled over. Then they could acknowledge the differences, and the two may have been able to problem solve by negotiation or compromise.

When problem solving, we can't criticize another's value system. Others value what they value. We value what we value. We can't shame another's value system as not viable, believable, or incorrect. In the next chapter, we'll discuss how to live in acceptance of another's value system, even though we don't agree with it. This is crucial.

Note: I am not endorsing accepting value systems that go against known society norms.

Defensive Responses

It is no surprise there were defensive responses between Anthony and Trever. Defensive responses are common when there's a felt need to justify a position. Our defensive responses usually come from a statement or action we did, a comparison to another's recent actions, a reminder of past infractions, a plea to listen to what's being said, and it goes on and on. Defensive responses hand an invitation over to the other person to respond defensively as well. Now, we're responding in a negative circle with no solution in sight.

One way to have a healthy conversation is to change our approach or how we enter into a discussion. For instance, using the words *curious* or *wondering* helps defuse many conversations. "I am curious about it. Can you tell me more?" "I am wondering if you need something from me, or do you just want me to listen." Eliminate all sentences starting with Why did you? Why didn't you? What were you thinking? Or other accusatory beginnings.

When we're at a stand still trying to prove ourselves right and the other wrong through defensive conversation, we're at a dead-end street. We have nowhere to go. There is no problem solving available. We only have arguments or declarations with defensive responses. After all, we are defending our values, and those beliefs can run deep within us.

The Spirit of Discontent

I'm grateful to a former pastor of mine for introducing me to the spirit of discontent. He gave a sermon about how, for ten years, he allowed discontentment to come into his life about another family member. I don't remember how he caught himself, but the point is, over time, he did. He identified this negative spirit and rejected it.

When a person allows negative, critical, and judgmental thoughts to enter in and build over time, it's likely the spirit of discontent is lurking around. Discontent means we feel dissatisfied, disgruntled, grieved, unhappy, resentful, frustrated, or irritated. It also means we've disengaged. These negative thoughts can be about a person, thing, or event. This spirit has resentments all in it, lots of victim and martyr thinking, plus fairness and justice issues. The spirit of discontent is full of tally marks like "I did this but you haven't done that." This spirit is bad news. Like resentments, we can justify these thoughts with all kinds of reasoning. Justified or not, the spirit of discontent is very destructive! It can create havoc and layers upon itself until we can't see anything positive anymore.

Unmet expectations, whether reasonable or unreasonable, can cause us to invite the spirit of discontent to enter in. In Philippians 4:12-13 the Apostle Paul talks about being content in all situations because of the strength God gives him.

"I know what it is the be in need, and I know what it is to have plenty. I have learned the secret of being content in any and every situation, whether well fed or hungry, whether living in plenty or in want. I can do everything in him who gives me strength."

In modern language, he knew God had his back! Start looking for the spirit of discontent in your life. You'll be surprised how often it shows up. When it shows up, reject it and pray the Lord will replace those thoughts with acceptance, contentment, and truth.

"Change your thoughts and you change your world."[xx]
-Norman Vincent Peale, minister, author

Dan allowed the spirit of discontent to come in. He allowed his legitimate disappointments to turn to discontent and resentment. We must watch that disappointment doesn't move us into the spirit of discontent because if we go there, we can barely get out of it. I'm always watching for it because it creeps in. The only solution is to recognize it and pray against it, and replace our negative thoughts with positive thoughts.

When Dan realized the spirit of discontent had taken hold of him, he used his wife, friends, and his faith to help him see what his true feelings were. He felt disappointed, blindsided, and betrayed. When we stay in our true emotions instead of allowing the spirit of discontent to come in, our faith, family, friends, and our community can help us work out the struggles within us. We have movement available to us in our true emotions. When we reside in discontent, we're shackled. If we ever feel lost, turn to Jeremiah 29:11-13 to remember God's promise to us.

"'For I know the plans I have for you," declares the Lord, "plans to prosper you and not to harm you, plans to give you hope and a future. Then you will call on me and come and pray to me, and I will listen to you. You will seek me and find me when you seek me with all your heart."

Legitimate Expectations

There are times we have a reasonable expectation because someone gave us an invitation, made a promise to us, or the expectation is part of our family culture. These expectations can be a neighbor inviting us over for dinner, someone promising to do something for us or our family, our children graduating from high school or college, our children getting a job, or someone following through with a promise made. Legitimate expectations can also include having a supportive boss or co-worker, neighbors taking care of their property, an elected official following through with their promises, as well as many others.

When expectations created by someone else fall through, it's disappointing or even devastating at times. I process these unmet expectations as disappointments, betrayals, or worse. They are usually just disappointments but can feel like betrayals. They need to be addressed before a resentment is formed. Voicing my disappointment to the appropriate person, without assuming they should know, is a healthy way to handle this.

When an expectation isn't met, it is unhealthy to assume why the expectation wasn't met. It's common to make negative assumptions when an expectation isn't met because it helps make sense of why we feel so badly. I want to blame someone or something to ease the pain. I can personalize the situation as against me. Assuming and personalizing words, actions, or situations by others can create havoc within me. This is because I only have the emotions, I don't have the facts. I'm assuming the facts. Check out the facts before making an assumption. We don't want the tension from a mistaken assumption.

There are other times when simple comments or questions are interpreted by others as an expectation. The speaker wasn't creating an expectation and is confused at the reaction of the other party. This type of miscommunication is very common and can create defensiveness and resentments from both parties as in the case below:

When James came home from work, Shanna asked if he was able to get some postage stamps on his way home.

James answered irritably, "The traffic was too heavy, it wasn't my fault."

Surprised and a little annoyed, Shanna responded, "I was just asking to see if I needed to go tomorrow. There was a possibility you could get them today. All I needed was a 'yes' or a 'no', so I can plan my day tomorrow."

James responded as if he had failed in a mission. He assumed Shanna had an expectation of him. She didn't. She was inquiring so she could plan her next day. It's best to refrain from answering defensively. Answer with clarification. "No, I didn't pick them up."

Expectations of Ourselves

We've discussed disappointments when expectations of others, things, and events don't materialize as we thought. We also place expectations upon ourselves and then face the same disappointments if they're not met. When we created the expectation, it seemed reasonable at the time. However, some expectations don't materialize, and we can be hard on ourselves. We become self-critical and allow shame to take over. Shame can be paralyzing. It leads to depression and discourages us from trying again. Let's look at a simple, everyday example.

Kelly is a thirty-three-year-old single mom. She balances a full-time job with her two young children. Kelly and her children live in an adequate apartment complex. Kelly's dream is to buy a house and raise her children in a good school district. She believed this is "what a good mother would do." After three years, Kelly is unable to move to the school district she decided was best for her children. She's beginning to believe she's not a good mother because she hasn't lived up to the expectations she created for herself.

Kelly joined a support group for single moms. She shared the frustrations and burden of being the only parent, the fatigue she felt most days, and other challenges a single mom of two young children would face.

She voiced, multiple times, she needed to figure out how she could buy a house and get her children into a good school district. Another group member voiced her opinion that some of Kelly's expectations were unrealistic given her situation.

When the group was over that night, Kelly was distraught over the group member's comment. She felt like she was misunderstood. Her mind kept repeating what she heard years ago, "living in a house and getting your children in a good school district is evidence of what a good mother would do." Kelly reasoned all single moms must feel this way. She made an appointment with the group facilitator to talk about her confusion and irritation over the other group member's comment. The facilitator asked Kelly to make a list of the "good" mothers she knows or has known and the characteristics of those "good" mothers.

Kelly wrote down the characteristics of the "good" mothers she knew. They were: openly affectionate; listens even when tired; tries to be patient; is responsive to the children's differences in thought, emotions, and behaviors; creates consistency but allows for spontaneity; sets reasonable boundaries; helps with homework, but doesn't enable; practices self-care.

Nowhere on the list was living in a house and getting her children into a good school district. Kelly was surprised by the outcome. Her definition of a good mother wasn't on the list. She was encouraged when she realized she had many attributes on that list.

Kelly's story is an example of misplaced or unrealistic expectations. She was hard on herself and felt defeated. Kelly continued in the group and continued to live in her apartment. She was able to hire a tutor for one of her children because she wasn't over extended by owning a house. She realized apartment living was less stressful than living in a house and she could give her children more attention.

Even though it took months for Kelly to realize she was, by her own definition, a "good" mother, she began to understand the problem of unrealistic expectations. Kelly set a standard she couldn't realistically meet because of the facts of her circumstances. She allowed the spirit of discontent to come in, and she looked outside of herself for her peace and contentment. Kelly helped others in the group learn how to evaluate and manage their expectations.

We often believe things should be better instead of choosing to be content. We stay unsettled and always wanting more. Discontent doesn't move us forward to live in REAL freedom. Realistic expectations and living in acceptance move us forward.

Managing Our Expectations

We now know a lot about expectations. We know if they aren't managed, there's trouble. Let's look at some suggestions for managing our expectations.

Ask these questions:

-What's happening because of my unmet expectations?

-Am I experiencing bitterness, unhappiness, discontent, or wanting to control?

-Am I expecting a person to value the same things I do?

-Am I stuck in trying to be right?

-Have I clearly communicated or heard correctly the expectations before me?

After we've considered these questions, we can use the reminders below to help manage our expectations:

-Trust in the larger picture. God knows what's going on.

-Resist victim or martyr thinking. It is like quicksand.

-Don't make secret contracts that are unknown to the other person.

-Clearly communicate your desires or expectations.

-Don't create unrealistic expectations for yourself or others.

-Remember other people cannot meet your core needs, only God can.

-Focus on Jeremiah 29:11-13 and Philippians 4:4-13.

Evaluating and managing our expectations is a process that brings us closer to living an emotionally and spiritually healthy life. Unrealistic expectations can fuel discord and resentments and don't provide the route to REAL freedom.

True freedom comes from releasing the things that keep us chained, which includes unrealistic and unhealthy expectations. Resentments and unrealistic expectations are like a ball and chain around our feet, dragging us through life. In the next chapter, we'll learn about acceptance and continue our understanding of why "it's me, not you," "it's us, not them," and the freedom this brings in all our relationships.

Evaluate Expectations Reflections are in the Appendix.

Chapter 6
Acceptance

Are you getting a taste of what healthy relationships look like? Are you beginning to see that "it's me, not you" is making more sense? This is such a better deal. We can have healthy relationships without the cooperation of anyone else. Sounds unreal but it is true. How?

Acceptance is another essential ingredient. Brian Tracy, a motivational speaker and author, agrees. He considers acceptance to be one of the greatest gifts we can give to others. And I add, to ourselves, as well.

> "The greatest gift that you can give to others is the gift of unconditional love and acceptance."[xxi]
> -Brian Tracy, motivational speaker and author

Acceptance is an interesting word. For me, it feels comfortable, but also challenging. It creates a sense of freedom, but also elicits mixed feelings. Most of the time, acceptance generates positive feelings and a positive state of mind. There is another side to acceptance that most of us don't consider but, is very powerful. A side that makes a huge difference in how we relate to others and to ourselves. This is what Ephesians 4 is about.

So, what is acceptance? Acceptance is commonly used when we affirm, support, tolerate or endure a situation, people, or events without requiring condoning or agreeing. Acceptance negates resistance. Acceptance can mean: I'm included, I'm going to college, my neighbors invited me over, I received an enthusiastic round of applause, they remembered my birthday. It can also mean: Even though I don't like it, he is who he is; I accept I need to let go of their recovery; I didn't make the cut and I accept it; I wish her values were different, but it's her choice.

In the healthy relationship world, acceptance has been called the gift that keeps on giving. Acceptance can be a complicated word, not because of its meaning but because of what's required of us. We are faced with accepting things or events every day. Sometimes I need to accept a situation or person I don't want to accept. This doesn't mean I approve or condone it. It means it is what it is, and I can't change it. The only recourse I have is to accept it and then figure out what I am going to do about it. This chapter isn't about working to be acceptable or popular. It's about living in REAL freedom and experiencing healthy relationships by learning the benefits acceptance brings.

Living in reality is the foundation for living in acceptance even if we don't approve or like the situation at hand. In our circle of family, friends, and co-workers, our different perspectives collide with each other's every day. We like to believe our view is correct or best, but it's just one interpretation out of many. What's best for me may not be best for you. The co-workers in the previous chapter witnessed the same accident but each processed it differently. Let's listen to, respect, and accept what others feel is true, even if we disagree. Remember our way of thinking is "a" way, not "the" way.

Does acceptance mean we have to like or approve what's going on or who someone is? No, acceptance is not condoning or altering our values. It doesn't mean we have to approve or like whatever reality is. We can be disappointed or sad, but the situation is still the same. Acceptance is just that - it is what it is.

The best part of acceptance is it gives us peace, confidence, and personal growth. It brings joy, contentment, and gratitude and opens the door to personal change and moving forward. It brings REAL freedom and helps us have REAL influence in all our relationships. Acceptance moves us from relying on our own resources for solving problems to healthy ways to solve problems. I think about it this way: Acceptance doesn't mean we change our values or beliefs. It means we don't require circumstances or people to be different and this frees us to make the decisions we need to make.

Acceptance and Expectations

Acquiring acceptance is central in releasing resentments and eliminating unreasonable or unrealistic expectations. Negativity and anxiety are reduced, health problems improve, personal peace is available, secret contracts and the *shoulds* disappear. Acquiring acceptance is tough, but it's necessary to develop and keep healthy relationships.

Acceptance minimizes our reactions to unmet expectations. We may have a spouse, sibling, co-worker, or other important relationship who thinks and does things differently than we do. When we're upset, they walk away. We want them to come closer and problem solve immediately, but they need time to think about it. They don't pick up on cues we think they should, but of course they don't - we never told them to.

Every day there are things that fall into this category. It's our job to accept the way others operate. We don't take it personally or criticize them because they don't see it the way we do. We can be disappointed or frustrated, but they are who they are, they do what they do. To repeat what I've said before, "don't let your sense of well-being be dependent on what someone does or doesn't do." Michael J. Fox puts it in words we can all understand.

"Happiness grows in direct proportions to my acceptance, and in inverse proportion to my expectations."[xxii]
-Michael J. Fox, Actor, Philanthropist

Acceptance and Family

We love our children, and from the day they were born, we start forming expectations for them. This results in many children living under the pressure, sometimes self-imposed, to be what they perceive their parents or family want them to be. They don't want to disappoint their family but also don't want to lose who they were created to be. Ed experienced this struggle. Here's his story:

"I was a compliant first born. Both my grandfathers were scientists. With this legacy and parental guidance which valued intelligence, tradition, hard work, and discipline – and definitely not the long-haired hippy fad I felt when I went to college - I should also study a science. I was told I was bright, and I guess that helped me struggle through. Ultimately, I acquired a science degree and graduated from a prestigious university.

I obtained a good job and became secure in my career. As long as I could remember, my desire was to be creative, not a scientist per se. I lived in a state of tension between creativity and practicality, between emotion and reason. Over the years, my tension began to ease by making room for hobbies. Since I was established with a good job at an excellent company, I was thankful for the support that ultimately helped me arrive at such a place in my life. I was able to spend creative time during my off-work hours.

A turning point came when my young family moved into a home with a basement, complete with an unfinished utility room, or as some say, "a cave." I turned part of our basement into a recording and sound studio, using the good job to make creativity more accessible.

In addition, I started studying photography and videography, as time permitted. I also started editing music to videos as a new hybrid form of expression. I was able to move past the expectations I felt when I was younger and move into who I knew I was created to be.

I'm someone who accepts that the bacon-bringing daily grind is reality, and I feel blessed I was able to incubate a few creative outlets on the side. I mean, it's quite an improvement from the serfdom of old when you think about it.

I was able to achieve all this without long term resentments because I decided to live in acceptance of who I am, how I got there, and how my grandparents and parents actually wanted the best for me. It was ultimately my responsibility to discover and embrace what my 'best' actually was. And really, what adult person expects their parents to have fully recognized or understood what would make their child happy in the future?"

Some adult children report they knew their parents or caregivers wanted the best for them, but their lack of acceptance made them feel like their parents didn't really like who they were. Adult children, even if considered successful, can still wonder if their parent or caregiver really likes or approve of them.

I've seen adults in their seventies still longing for approval from their parent who's in their nineties. This was my mom's story. She was a good caregiver to her mother. It was hard to watch how my grandmother treated her. I asked my grandmother why she won't tell her daughter, my mother, that she loved her. My grandmother scoffed and said, "She should know. I shouldn't have to tell her." My heart broke.

Accepting our children for who they are is critical. Resisting who they are can have long lasting negative consequences. Embrace your children, encourage them, set boundaries, but above all accept them! It's a gift that lasts forever.

Ed's story could have had a difficult ending. Parents or caregivers want to guide children so they don't make obvious mistakes. At the same time, they need to accept who their children are, not want they them to be. The parents' or caregivers' position can force the child to go against what the child knows is true for themselves.

Accepting your children for who they are and what they want to be can be hard but rewarding. It may mean grieving the loss of who we thought our children would be. However, even though it's hard, acceptance can result in our children becoming free to be who they are created to be. They can lead a healthy life without regret.

Ed's story illustrates his struggle and ultimate decision to accept and make the best of his situation. His decisions produced positive results, created space for problem solving, and promoted living in REAL freedom and having REAL influence in his relationships for years.

Most of us have family members other than our children. Some relationships are easy, and some are difficult to tolerate. If our relatives were our neighbors, we may not choose to be their friend. Family relationships are here to stay. We need to accept it and work on it. Let's see how Tim handled a difficult family relationship.

Tim and his wife, Donna, were watching a movie with a storyline that revealed a possible solution to one of Tim's recurring struggles.

"You know, honey, the movie triggered the feelings I still have about Jack. I wish we connected better as brothers. Anne seems to do fine with him, but there's something missing in my relationship with him. I've tried many approaches. When he criticizes me, I've pushed back, I've not pushed back, I've tried to engage, I've not engaged, nothing seems to work."

"I know, you've tried, but Jack is different. He sees things with a different set of lenses. My guess is he has no idea you feel dismissed or criticized by him. You've tried to let Jack know how you feel, but I think you two talk a different language and come from a different point of view. I think you expect Jack to be like you, but he's not."

"I realize I'm the troubled one, I don't think Jack is. So, I guess I'm the one who needs to figure this out," sighed Tim.

"Anne told me your brother is who he is and isn't going to change. She's learned to accept Jack for who he is and how he operates. She said she doesn't have certain expectations of him and doesn't feel hurt or disappointed anymore."

"Jack has a need to teach, instruct, and dominate our conversations. He has to be right. All these years, I've never figured out what to do."

"The movie suggested doing nothing but accepting who he is, how he sees and does things. I know you don't like some of Jack's traits, but that's Jack. He probably feels he's being helpful in his conversations with you. He may enjoy enlightening you and doesn't perceive himself as instructing and demanding."

Tim felt motivated to end this dilemma once and for all. He decided to accept his brother and let go of the unrealistic expectation that Jack be someone he isn't. It took time, but Tim was successful in developing healthy and realistic expectations. A wonderful side product was he finally released the resentments he had toward Jack. He was free.

Tim chose to accept Jack's disposition and personality instead of waiting for his brother to change. This acceptance enabled him to enjoy the brother relationship he longed for, even though it didn't match the picture he imagined. It may seem unfair Tim had to do all the emotional work; however, Tim was the one with the longings and disappointments. He imagined what their relationship *should* look like and was continually disappointed. Remember the land of the *shoulds* in the expectations chapter? They aren't the answer here.

Is this the outcome Tim wanted? No, but it's an honest one. Tim's awareness and internal struggle pointed to the fact he's the one to look for a solution. Will Tim ever be disappointed with Jack? Absolutely, however, his acceptance of Jack allows him to move on, limit topics to talk about, and agree to disagree. Tim was the one who struggled, so, he was the one to look for a solution.

When Jack tries to instruct or enlighten him, Tim thanks him for the input and then does what he believes is best for himself even if there is subsequent criticism or push-back from Jack. This is not done in spite but in the spirit of accepting his brother for who he is and staying true to himself.

Since his brother was oblivious to all this, it was Tim who had to adjust his expectations. Is there sadness here? Yes. Does it seem unfair? Yes. Is there a resentment? Not now. Is there acceptance? Yes. Is there REAL freedom? Yes! Is he able to have REAL influence in his relationship?

Does Tim have a healthy relationship with Jack? Most would say "no," but he does. This is the tricky part. Even a one-way relationship can be healthy. That's why "it's me, not you." Tim chose to accept the only relationship Jack had to offer. He tried to make it different, but Jack didn't go along with it.

Tim accepted this was all he was going to get. He chose to relate to Jack in the only way Jack would relate. He chose the healthy path even though he was disappointed. Tim feels free, he isn't thinking about what he could do differently to change his brother. Jack is Jack.

Accepting Others

Jesus modeled acceptance. He approached people for who they were and what they were doing. He accepted the rich, poor, infirmed, broken, faithful, and unfaithful. He even demonstrated acceptance when He challenged the Pharisees. This doesn't mean He agreed with them. He accepted who they were and how they operated, so He spoke to them with that understanding. The Pharisees spoke from the literal interpretation of the law while Jesus spoke from the spiritual interpretation of the law, which most of the Pharisees didn't accept. We need to be this understanding when faced with different perspectives with family, friends, and co-workers.

After Christ's resurrection, many Jewish Christians found it difficult to accept the increasing number of Gentile Christians. They weren't doing things right. They lived different lifestyles. They ate unclean food. Acts 15 records the discussions about how to accept and integrate these Gentile Christians. The bottom line is found in Acts 15:8, as Peter explained to the others, "God, who knows the heart, showed he accepted them by giving the Holy Spirit to them, just as he did to us." The Lord's graciousness was obvious to all.

It's so awesome for God to use the Holy Spirit to bind us together. If I were there and witnessed this incredible scene of acceptance, I hope I would have embraced it. So, how can we use this scene today? What do we need to change within us?

This is one reason Ephesians 4 is the cornerstone of this book - the acceptance of the gentiles and the instructions that came along with it.

I, like many others, struggle with acceptance. I continue to work on it. There's a part of me that doesn't want to accept another's point of view because I just don't want to. I feel I'm right, or at least my perspective is better. I may be right for myself, but it doesn't mean I'm right for others and how they process situations. Just because I believe I'm right doesn't change the dynamic or situation.

When living in acceptance, being right is irrelevant. The key is to accept the differences, compromise, and problem solve. What do you need to change to live in acceptance, like the disciples had to do with the new Christians' bad habits and ways of living?

Most of us understand Tim's struggle with his brother. There's nothing wrong with the desire that someone or something be different. If it causes us distress and we try to change someone, it's a negative approach to the problem. It's not productive. Acceptance and healthy boundaries are the answer to experiencing healthy relationships, even though there might be disappointment.

"Happiness can exist only in acceptance."[xxiii]
-George Orwell, Author

Accepting Ourselves

Most of us know we need to love and accept others. However, we can be sketchy about loving and accepting ourselves. Matthew 22:35-40 (NLT) explains how important it is to love others and ourselves.

"One of them, an expert in religious law, tried to trap him with this question: 'Teacher, which is the most important commandment in the law of Moses?' Jesus replied, 'You must love the Lord your God with all your heart, all your soul, and all your mind. This is the first and greatest commandment. A second is equally important: Love your neighbor as yourself. The entire law and all the demands of the prophets are based on these two commandments.'"

When we read or repeat this well-known verse, we often concentrate on the command to love others. But notice, the verse says love our neighbor as (we love) ourselves. This implies to love our neighbor, we need to love ourselves.

Accepting ourselves can be hard. Sure, we make mistakes and do some things we'd like to take back. When I think of one of mine, I still shudder. "What was I thinking?" Give ourselves the gift of kindness and forgiveness. It's the path to freedom. When we make mistakes, it doesn't mean we don't have value anymore, it means we are human and need to give ourselves grace and mercy.

An aubergine cartoon I came across a few years ago, inspired the vignette below:

Mr. Cabbage noticed Mr. Eggplant appeared depressed and asked him what was wrong.

"I'm sad I can't be sold in an egg carton. Every day, every hour, shoppers buy egg cartons with 12 or more eggs in it."

"As much as you may want to be, you will never be sold in an egg carton," the friendly head of cabbage told him.

"Why can't I?" sighs the eggplant.

"Because you're an eggplant, you're not an egg, and you won't fit. You are a vegetable; you're bigger and you don't taste like those eggs in the egg carton. People find you extraordinary!"

"Really? It's sounds like I'm special in a different way."

"Yes," explains Mr. Cabbage, "you're bought individually for who you are, not part of a group of 12 or 18."

"Wow! I never thought about it like that, it sounds like I'm unique."

"You are!"

"This is a great day, thank you Mr. Cabbage."

I am not Mr. Cabbage, but I am here to say we are all God's masterpieces. He wants us to accept and live in this truth. Accept ourselves as he accepts us.

It's healthy to accept ourselves even if we're disappointed in ourselves. We can offer ourselves kindness. We can pray or run it by other people, even if we are embarrassed to do so. Forgiving and being kind to ourselves is our responsibility. If we stay too long in disappointment, shame takes over and we start to beat ourselves up.

Unhealthy Shame

Feeling guilty about something is okay as long as we take action to right a wrong or ask for forgiveness. If we avoid this type of resolution, we sentence ourselves to sit in shame. Staying in shame is unhealthy. This is a fluid process, and we need to stay vigilant to not let shame come in. Shame can be paralyzing and has no redeeming value except to motivate us to right a wrong. If we don't use it for this purpose, we will have a hard time accepting ourselves.

There is healthy and unhealthy shame. I first heard this when I took some training at Open Hearts Ministry currently in Grand Rapids, Michigan. Healthy shame is when something happens that requires an apology or reparations. This shame or guilt propels us to right the wrong. We do what is required, we are forgiven, and we let go.

Unhealthy shame is when we keep thinking about what we've done even after being forgiven. We continue to beat ourselves up. We ruminate and play the situation over and over. Other unhealthy shame comes from things we imagine people are thinking or saying about us. It's not founded on anything concrete or provable, but we make it real in our minds. Unhealthy shame is paralyzing.

Some people believe sitting in shame is an action to help right the wrong or is somehow admirable, but it isn't. There is no redeeming value in unhealthy shame. Jesus took our shame. He took it to his death and resurrection.

Controlling and Demanding

I'm fairly active with my family and my community. When I'm on a committee or trying to work out a solution for something, I often believe I see things clearer than most. I might, but not always. There was a time I stepped in too often to offer my advice. Looking back, it seems like I couldn't help myself. I thought I needed to step in and inform others or make it happen the way I thought it should happen. We touched on this in the expectations chapter.

I'd analyze the situation and decide how I could help them change things. I didn't recognize it was my perspective but might not be theirs. I didn't see my actions as demanding or controlling. I saw my actions as helpful, as the best solution. Everyone will be grateful. Really? I was pretty arrogant and disrespectful, I now realize.

Until I caught myself, I was okay with this position. I don't want others to make mistakes or poor choices like I've done. Since I believed I was thoughtful and kind, I spent more energy than I should trying to change this person, thing, or event. I justified my position because I believed it was for their good. I was definitely not in acceptance.

What I was doing was trying to make reality into what I thought it should be, but clothed it in the helping and caring trump card. It's hard to challenge someone for their controlling or demanding behavior when they say this is their way of showing how much they care. This is a tough concept for some of us to accept because we believe more in our good intentions than others saying we are controlling. When others are inserting themselves, the hardest ones to convince are those who say they prayed about it or experienced something similar. It sounds good, but is it a justification to control? These can be the most difficult ones to decipher.

When we're honest and start removing the layers created by our controlling tendencies, we'll see our own arrogance, disrespect, and fear are the root of this behavior. This can be confusing for people who think they are "just helping." They see themselves as caring so much and they want what is best for the person or the situation. One of my favorite verses is appropriate here:

> "Trust in the Lord with all your heart and lean not on your own understanding; in all your ways submit to him, and he will make your paths straight." Proverbs 3:5-6.

Ask the Lord what he's really asking you to do. Our job is to accept people for who they are just as God accepts us for who we are, flaws and all. Let's further explore acceptance in the next chapter. It will tell us what it means and how to acquire acceptance.

Acceptance Reflections are in the Appendix.

Chapter 7
Acquire Acceptance

When we acquire acceptance and decide to step back and do nothing, we're most likely responding in a healthy way. This is moving forward. Tim was able to move forward because he finally accepted his brother for who he is. When we accept, we have choices for how we react. If a person is difficult, we call it as we see it and create boundaries. We don't have to try and change or enlighten them. Trying to change someone bogs us down. Let's be free.

Acceptance and Resistance

If I'm not in acceptance, I'm usually in resistance. Resistance can show up in many parts of our life. Remember Dan from the expectations chapter? His expectations for his new workplace weren't met. He started comparing his new location to his old location and became discontented. He was living in resistance of his actual circumstances, his new reality. We all experience resistance at one time or another. We need to recognize it and find a way out of it.

What is resistance? Resistance is a negative or judgmental feeling we have toward ourselves, others, things, or events. We want something to be different, someone to be different, or our life to be different. When we are in resistance, we can't accept or go along with something or someone. It can be an action, a conversation or a comment.

Sometimes reality shows us a picture we don't want. If we need to operate within that picture at home or on the job, we can become discontented. We don't like the picture. We resist the picture. We ruminate about what or how the picture should look.

We try to come up with solutions to change the picture. When these efforts are futile, we operate out of resistance and discontent, and this further frustrates us. We stay in resistance and refuse to move into acceptance because we think acceptance might mean approving or condoning things we don't like. If I'm able to make reality different because it's in my realm of responsibility, then fine. If it's not my responsibility, I need to back out.

Common statements indicating we're operating outside our realm of responsibility are: "I told her so many times and she does just the opposite." "I give, give, give and get no appreciation." "I bought them _____ and they aren't even using it." "Why can't they change, why are they like that?" "What a waste." "Where did they get that idea." "What is wrong with them?" "Can't they see the right answer? Can't they see the right way to do this?" "I need to tell them how they should do this or that." "I need to call their _____ and see if they can help with this situation." "I have told them over and over the right way to do this or think about this."

Resisting what is actually true or who someone is won't move us forward. Acceptance is what moves us forward. We suffer more when we're in resistance. We have few options, and we're ripe for resentments, unrealistic expectations, thinking like a victim or a martyr, or becoming demanding and controlling. This produces an invitation for the spirit of discontent to arrive on the scene again. We don't want this visitor. If we aren't living in acceptance, we're probably living in resistance. Resistance is like an ill-fitting pair of shoes, pinching and creating blisters; keeping us agitated and discontented. Acceptance is like spending the day on a beautiful beach dancing barefoot in the soft sand and humming a happy tune!

Resistance blocks us from experiencing REAL freedom and having REAL influence in our relationships. It blocks peace, joy, contentment, and the ability to have healthy relationships. When we're in resistance we may be analyzing night and day and allowing resentments, bitterness, and the spirit of discontent to come in. If you find you are often in resistance, pray, journal, talk with a friend, read an uplifting novel or devotional. If it continues and creates problems, you may want to get professional help. Use Ephesians 4:1-3 as your goal.

> "As a prisoner for the Lord, then, I urge you to live a life worthy of the calling you have received. Be completely humble and gentle; be patient, bearing with one another in love. Make every effort to keep the unity of the Spirit through the bond of peace."

Acceptance is relating in the positive. It's a good thing. Acceptance means I'm accepting this is what it is - this is reality. Even though I don't like it or approve of it and it can hurt or disappoint me, I still acknowledge and accept it. When we are in acceptance positive results are available, but they are limited in resistance, or doesn't even exist. Trying to make changes from a position of resistance and discontentment rarely works because we are using negative energy and taking the problem into our own hands.

"What you resist not only persists, but will grow in size."[xxiv]
-Carl Jung, Psychologist

Acceptance and Problem Solving

We're asked to accept many things, our feelings, needs, desires, choices, where we and others are in life. We are also asked to accept relationships, problems, blessings, financial status, where we live, where we work, and many other things. Sometimes we don't want to accept these things. This is another place resistance takes hold. We may not recognize it at first, because the resistance feels justifiable. True problem solving is not likely in resistance. Healthy problem solving is available in acceptance. Acceptance is the door to problem solving. Remember acceptance is not condoning or agreeing, it's reality.

Acquiring acceptance doesn't mean we do nothing, become passive, or get walked over. It gives us healthy options, listed earlier, to be able to navigate and live in acceptance of undesirable situations. Acceptance also reduces inner conflict about what we're experiencing and offers more personal peace so we can get back to living our own life. Acceptance instead of resistance means any action we take is non-reactive and comes from a place of thoughtfulness, flexibility, and truth instead of from a place of defensiveness, anger, or being closed off. This is what makes problem solving work.

Benefits of Acquiring Acceptance

When we acquire acceptance, we're living in the freedom God intended for us. We become new, we become free, we enjoy life.

> "You were taught, with regard to your former way of life, to put off your old self, which is being corrupted by its deceitful desires; to be made new in the attitude of your minds; and to put on the new self, created to be like God in true righteousness and holiness."
> -Ephesians 4:22-24

We can't change something until we first accept it. Acceptance brings about patience, tolerance, thoughtfulness, and compassion instead of anger and resentment. It brings about peace and contentment instead of discontentment, even if we're disappointed, sad, or worried. Acceptance comes from a place of kindness and love instead of demanding and shaming.

Acceptance gives us choices. Instead of allowing annoying behaviors to get to us, we accept the person's behaviors are annoying and are free to decide what we'll do about it. This is such a great statement. It's the opposite of how most of us live.

We can decide to limit our time with some people or avoid certain conversational topics. We make these choices in the spirit of acceptance, not in the spirit of discontent, resistance, anger, or judgment. With acceptance we don't need to try and change someone or something. We just accept them. It is what it is. They are who they are. Henry Wadsworth Longfellow figured this out long ago through this analogy.

"For after all, the best thing one can do
when it is raining is let it rain."[xxv]
-Henry Wadsworth Longfellow, Poet and Educator

With acceptance, we can choose to say "yes," or "no," or to do nothing. We can take our anger and disappointment to God or to our trusted friends to help us get through whatever we are going through. We can make healthy decisions for ourselves. We can distance ourselves from others for a period of time. We can mind our own business. We can actually live in peace and joy even with disappointments. We can ask if our help or perspective is needed, or wanted, and then accept the answer. What freedom! As I'm writing this paragraph, I feel lighter and joyful. It's like a weight lifting off me. This is another reminder that I have healthy options and options are good.

When I choose acceptance, I have movement. I can change, I'm free, and I don't have a ball and chain weighing me down. Acceptance means any action I take comes from a thought-out and prayerful position. It's non-reactive and comes from a place of power, flexibility, and truth instead of from a place of controlling, defensiveness, and negativity. Acceptance is a balm to our soul.

We can accept ourselves even if we're disappointed with ourselves. We can offer ourselves kindness and understanding. We can pray or run it by other people even if we're hesitant or afraid to do so. Forgiving and being kind to ourselves is our responsibility. If we stay too long in disappointment, shame takes over. As we've discussed, staying in shame is an unhealthy negative approach.

Acceptance and Everyday Problems

What about acceptance of ordinary things or events? We're in a long line or bad traffic. We accidently show up two hours late at a gathering. We get partnered with someone we don't know. We're not invited to a neighbor's party. We're blindsided by comments a friend made. Acquiring acceptance helps us decide if we can do something about it or not. Resistance invites irritation and resentment. Living in acceptance keeps us reasonable and able to plan instead of feeling out of control from our negativity, hurt, or disappointment. It frees us to pray with integrity instead of praying with a demanding or victim spirit.

What about disappointments with family members? We read Ed's letter and gained a certain perspective from him. Periodic disappointment with family members happens. Sometimes we understand why and sometimes we don't. Acceptance is still the answer. As we mentioned earlier, we may need to mourn the loss of what we wanted a family member to be instead of taking the unhealthy route of trying to change them. This is an impossible task anyway.

Living in resistance of who our family member is distorts our perceptions and distracts us from what is going right. Accepting our family member for who he or she is allows us to adjust how we will relate to them. Will we set better boundaries? Will we limit our time with them? Will we not loan them money? These are other examples of "it's me, not you." We are free to make healthy decisions for ourselves. We are relating in a healthy way even if the other person isn't.

One of the hardest things to accept is injustice and things that happen to our children, friends, and our family. Jesus modeled that for us. He took the greatest injustice but didn't rebel. Did he ask for it to be taken away? Yes. Did his friends let him down when he needed them? Yes. Yet he looked to his Father to get him through. As we learned earlier, ask the Lord to help you get through your difficulty – not get out of or get rid of it, but through it.

Acceptance contributes to a calmer, more contented life. If we don't practice being content, we open the door to the spirit of discontent, which then invites us to act like toddlers throwing a fit on the floor. Not a pleasant sight.

Acceptance is living REAL. It's living a relationally healthy life based on reality and truth. Resisting basically says we want to live our life in fantasy – a life we want, but a life that isn't REAL. Living in acceptance is relating to others in truth. It's living a life with love, positivity, healthy boundaries, and healthy consequences. Life becomes more enjoyable with acceptance. It becomes a life God designed instead of one we designed. If your desire is to live a simpler and more realistic life, live in acceptance.

Will we experience disappointment when we live in acceptance? Yes. Will we feel some anger or sadness while we're trying to live in acceptance? Again, absolutely, but it's worth it. Acceptance and contentment are like BFFs (best friends forever). There is fun, there is security, there is hope, and there is a future.

The benefits of living in acceptance are extraordinary. Below are some suggestions to help you work through and stay in acceptance:

- -Accept what's been given to you (that doesn't mean you have to like it).
- -Trust in the larger picture.
- -Enjoy who people are and enjoy who you are.
- -Live in reality, not what you want reality to be.
- -Make hard decisions.
- -Don't try to change people, change only what you are responsible for.
- -Trust where and who you are today is exactly where you're supposed to be.
- -Trust where and who others are today is exactly where they're supposed to be.
- -Remember, what you resist persists!
- -Choose healthy relating in all your relationships.

-Remember, it's me, not you that needs to do the work or it's us, not them.

Pray the full Serenity Prayer:

God, give me grace to accept with serenity the things that cannot be changed,

Courage to change the things which should be changed,

And the Wisdom to distinguish the one from the other.

Living one day at a time, enjoying one moment at a time,

Accepting hardship as a pathway to peace, taking, as Jesus did,

This sinful world as it is, not as I would have it,

Trusting that You will make all things right,

If I surrender to Your will, so that I may be reasonably happy in this life,

And supremely happy with You forever in the next. Amen.-

Niebuhr[xxvi]

Acceptance gives us REAL freedom, peace, and influence in all our relationships. We feel settled and can think clearer. Our relationships are healthy even if they are one-way. We can relax and have fun because we relate respectfully and problem solve more frequently. Our joy returns, and life feels lighter. Acquiring acceptance helps us move into our next and important chapter, *Letting Go.*

Acquire Acceptance Reflections are in the Appendix.

Chapter 8
Letting Go

We are close to fully equipping ourselves to live relationally healthy. This is great. We've covered a lot in the previous chapters. Now, letting go is the final key ingredient. We have seen the value of releasing Resentments, evaluating Expectations, acquiring Acceptance, and now it's time to learn to Let go. Letting go of people, places, thoughts, and habits is next. Only you know who or what they are. What you've experienced in the other chapters is a guidepost.

Are you struggling with the idea of letting go of someone or something? Does it feel scary, uncomfortable, or not fair? I used to feel like I would lose something if I let go. What that something was, I'm not sure. It just felt like a loss and possibly an unfair loss.

In general conversations, we often say, "I really need to let that go." But do we mean it? Meaning and doing don't always match up. It is healthy to know you need to let go of something or someone, but the follow through…that's another story. Deciding to follow through can seem like there's too much to it. There's fear or worry it might not work out or we will make a mistake. This chapter is here to let you know there is a healthy letting go. It's not easy but the end results are amazing.

What is Letting Go?

We may know we need to let go, but we don't know what it looks like. Letting go occurs when we are no longer anxious, burdened with, or holding onto something or someone. We may be confused or hurt, but we don't let it dominate our life.

Letting go allows us to redirect our thoughts and actions to what we need to be looking at, thinking about, and responding to. This shift moves us into the freedom we long for and are created for. It gives us the freedom needed to move us along in our personal and spiritual growth. When we let go, we release negativity, we understand others' perspectives, we problem solve, and we experience gratitude and peace. It's also the realization if we don't let go, we've put ourselves in a cage. A cage we are unaware of but need to get out of because it keeps us stuck. Stuck because we hold on to people things and events we need to let go of. So, how do we do this letting go?

What's Involved in Letting Go?

The benefits of letting go are unique to each person. We no longer ruminate or overthink things. We don't spend hours thinking about and plotting how to fix something or someone. We don't personalize someone else's problem as ours. We let go of what we want reality to be and accept what reality is. We let go of "they should know better and I need to tell them." We adjust communication that sounds controlling even if we believe we are being caring or concerned. We realize others have different views, values, and solutions that are different from ours. We don't try to save the world or our family and friends. Our overthinking and replaying of events and conversations stop or are greatly minimized, and we sleep better at night.

When I don't have a clear-cut resolution with someone or something, I find letting go is hard. I like resolution. After years of trying to force some resolutions, I understand, with some situations, there may never be a resolution. That's one reason this book continues to focus on what we can do about our situations and relationships. It's not about waiting for others to do or not do something.

When I let go, I am releasing people and things and setting myself free from all the disappointments, betrayals, ruminations, misunderstandings, negative feelings, and others too numerous to list. Letting go isn't always about letting go of negative things. We need to let go of people and things we love but hold onto too tightly.

When someone has a problem, we may think analyzing, planning, and creating solutions for them is being supportive. The number one rule is to ask if our help is needed. If we don't ask and they don't ask us, let it go. We can pray instead.

I know I can work myself up with too much overthinking about someone's problems, because I want them to know how concerned I am. I need to release the anxiety I create when I'm not appreciated for all the concern and good answers I might have for someone's problem. The bottom line is I need to let go of getting into someone else's business unless I'm asked.

One problem is, some of us think our ruminating and overthinking shows our concern. We can show concern in other ways. For some, this seems to go against everything we've been taught - we should always be there for others. We need to reframe this. What if not doing anything is the healthiest way of being there for others?

Now that I trust the process of letting go, I see it calms, frees, and uplifts me. It also brings me into new spaces. Peaceful spaces. Can you do it? Can you set yourself free? When we choose to let go, we reduce the risk of losing what we've learned about addressing resentments, expectations, and acceptance. If we don't let go, we're prone to be depressed, angry, resentful, unforgiving, and revert back to our old ways. I know, I don't want to do that.

Do you want to free yourself like freeing animals from their cages or do you want to keep holding on? By the end of these last two chapters, my hope is you will become free from the encumbrances holding on brings. Letting go gives us the ticket to develop healthy relationship and enjoy REAL freedom and have REAL influence in all our relationships.

> "Some people believe holding on and hanging in there are signs of great strength. However, there are times when it takes much more strength to know when to let go and then do it."[xxvii]
> -Ann Landers, Columnist

Did We Build Ourselves a Cage?

If we did, let's free ourselves. Resentments, unmanaged expectations, resisting acceptance, and not letting go are the materials we used to build the cage. What's the name of your cage and what benefit are you receiving? Can you open the door, go out, and enjoy your freedom? If not, are you comfortable in a cage because you don't know how or are afraid to live with REAL freedom?

We may not realize we're caged so we decide to stay inside thinking we're in a safe place. Does your cage have a dart board with people's faces on it or contain a storehouse of resentments and grief?

Do we believe we need to stay in our cage because leaving it might mean we have to repair a relationship we don't want to repair, or leaving might mean someone will never have to pay, or someone will never know how much they hurt us? Let go, step out, and be free. It's in you. You have the courage. You can do it.

Benefits of Leaving Our Cage

Leaving our cage also means we don't ruminate or replay events or conversations. We let go of the need to hear remorse or an apology. We seek good counsel when we feel lost. We seek help to heal deep wounds. We have choices and choices are always good. We are free, and this is good news.

Leaving our cage also means we no longer personalize someone's poor judgment or tactlessness. We refrain from trying to fix someone or insert ourselves into another's problem without being asked. We let go of the need to inform people they "should know better." We let go of unresolved past hurts. We embrace compassion for ourselves. We settle with the past and look toward to the future. This is all good stuff, but it takes work on our part.

We know what we need to let go of, but sometimes it's been around so long letting go feels like we lost and someone else won or we are losing part of the familiar, part of our identity. When we let go, we are establishing our new self. We accept reality for what it is, not what we want it to be. Is this difficult? It can be, but this is what truly sets us free. We voluntarily stepped into our cage because we thought it would protect us and keep us safe in our relationships, but it doesn't. Letting go is what works. Open those doors. Release your resentments, unmanaged expectations, and unacceptance. Step out into freedom.

As a prisoner, himself, Nelson Mandela knows about letting go.

"As I walked out the door toward the gate that would
lead to my freedom, I knew if I didn't leave my bitterness
and hatred behind, I'd still be in prison."[xxviii]
-Nelson Mandela, Former president of South Africa,
Activist/Prisoner

Getting Through It

Someone close to me, who I call Chris, hurt me deeply. The impact was agonizing. I felt betrayed, blindsided, foolish, misunderstood, and many other deep emotions. Chris didn't seem to understand the depth of my hurt. There was acknowledgement I was hurt but uninterest or unwillingness to know how deep the hurt was. I wanted Chris to know. Certainly, I would feel better if Chris knew the depth of the hurt!

I built and entered my own cage, waiting for someone to release me. I sat there for a long time. Chris had no idea about the cage or the "responsibility" to release me.

During this time, my daily routine was to read a chapter from the Bible and a daily reading from *The Language of Letting Go* by Melody Beattie[xxviv]. On March 15, she wrote:

"It's not whether others see that we're hurt, it is whether we see and care about how hurt we are."

I didn't understand and was fairly sure I didn't want to. It sounded like my feelings were my responsibility and I needed to let go of something I felt I deserved. It was hard to accept those words, but I knew this important message was for me.

After rolling it around in my head for about four months, I had an incredible "ah ha" moment. I remember exactly where I was and what I was doing when it finally made sense to me.

Of course, I'm the one who needs to know how hurt I am because I'm the only one who knows what I need when this hurt comes flooding in. Duh! Do I need to pray, call a friend, get a massage, go for a walk, see a movie, read scripture or a favorite book?

I accepted I was the only one I can count on to take care of my hurt. I let go of the expectation that Chris needed to know. My hurt and disappointment belong to me, and I can take care of them. I have other possibilities than hurt and disappointment. Wow, but do I want to? Do I want to let go knowing Chris will never know how hurt I was? "Yes," I decided, "I want to be free." So, I stepped out of the cage and started the process of letting go.

This worked for a while. Months later, I put a few toes back into my cage. My desire for Chris to know how much I was hurt came creeping back. "Okay," I thought, "I know Chris will never know how much I hurt, but surely on the death bed, there will be reflection and understanding. Chris will be remorseful." I was content with this for about five years, believing the remorse would happen, if only on the death bed. I really tidied this one up and stepped back into my cage, until that fateful day when the truth stared me straight in the face. If a person doesn't know or care how hurt you are in life, it's not going to happen on their death bed.

I moved on. I let go. This time I was truly free. There won't be a death bed experience. I was no longer tied to this need to have someone realize how much they hurt me. I'm the only one who needs to know. I'm the only one who can take care of me. I'm the only one who needs to have compassion for me. Not only did I step out of my cage, I destroyed it. Wow! What freedom! This process was one of the most defining moments in my life. This is a good example of what "it's me, not you" means. I'm the one who can set myself free. Chris was clueless.

C. S. Lewis, British author and lay theologian, backs this up with his wisdom:

> "Getting over a painful experience is much like crossing monkey bars. You have to let go at some point in order to move forward."xxx

Expectations and Letting Go

Letting go also includes letting go of certain expectations we have of ourselves and others. In the expectation chapters, we learned we can get caught in the *shoulds*—deciding what *should* happen or not happen, who we *should* be, or who others *should* be. Getting into the *shoulds* is like getting into quicksand, you slowly and painfully sink down until you no longer exist. Don't let the *shoulds* in. Run. Get away, let go, be free.

As we've learned, it is important to evaluate and manage our expectations, and to accept reality. This allows us to let go of those things that aren't realistic, not our business, or aren't healthy. Unmanaged expectations can bog us down by expecting things from others we didn't clearly communicate (secret contracts). We can have unrealistic expectations of our own performance, competency, and our basic need to be appreciated and liked. Letting go of unrealistic expectations about ourselves or others is necessary, even if we're disappointed if they don't materialize.

When letting go, I need to ask these questions: Do I need to step down from a responsibility? Do I need to let go of being important? Do I need to say no? Do I need to say yes? Do I need to stop worrying about what other people think? Do I feel pulled to do something, even though my gut is saying no? Do I feel selfish if I'm taking care of myself? These and similar questions can alert us to what's preventing us from making the bold step of letting go. Let's see how Albert and Cynthia wrestled with it.

At their favorite restaurant, Albert and Cynthia were glad to have a night out. However, Albert seemed detached.

Cynthia noticed, "Are you distracted tonight because of the Community Club?"

"I'm not sure. Some days I feel I shouldn't run for a second term as president, and then I change my mind. I'm afraid the Club won't be the same. I initiated some good programs, and they've asked me to stay another year."

"I know. You've done a wonderful job, but our family situation is different this year. We need you. Don't worry, you will always be known as the first Community Club president."

"You're right. I need to decide. I'm supposed to submit names for the other positions in two weeks."

Albert believed his skill set was valuable and the Club needed him to continue as president. Even though his gut was saying to step down, he was still struggling.

"What if discord develops or our membership drops because I'm not there? What if the new president doesn't care like I do, and the meetings get out of hand?"

Many of us, like Albert, are afraid to let go of things near and dear to us, but there's a time and place to let go and move on. This was Albert's time. It was hard. Albert was holding on to his importance too tightly and didn't trust the potential changes. Even though his gut was saying not to run, he found it difficult to let go and hand his responsibilities to someone else.

"Honey, trust the process and believe in the bigger picture. Yes, there may be bumps along the road, but the Club will recover. Can you be okay even if the picture looks different than you think it should be?"

In Albert's case, letting go is not shutting down or walking away. It's concluding he needs to release control to others at the appropriate time.

When we're experiencing changes in our lives, it may signal it's time to let go of the now and move toward the future. Letting go is a healthy way to keep us in the present, accept reality, and redefine our priorities.

I faced this reality years ago. I needed to step down from the Director of Women's Ministry position, a position I loved. The ministry was thriving, we added more activities, and the attendance was up and continued to grow. But like Albert, my family needed me to resign. I struggled with it. I was concerned whether the recent changes would stay and if the ministry would continue to thrive.

I did resign. The ministry changed some, but I trusted our committee. I was sad for a while, but it was the best decision. The transition was fine, and I celebrated with them.

Acceptance and Letting Go

In the *Acquire Acceptance* chapter, we watched Tim struggle to accept his brother, Jack, and how he viewed things and operated relationally. Tim learned to let go of trying to change Jack as well as his need for Jack's approval. He became confident within himself and now enjoyed being around his brother.

"Do I lose myself when I let go?" A good question, but no, it's quite the opposite. With letting go we're establishing and clarifying what our attitudes, values, and behaviors are. We're not trying to force them on someone or something. Instead, we're standing firm within ourselves and making healthy choices when confronted with attitudes, values, and behaviors we don't agree with.

The title, *It's Me, Not You*, encourages readers to understand how healthy relationships start and stop with us, no one else. Relationships where we use appropriate boundaries, resist unhealthy conflict, and use the REAL formula. This frees us to live without resentments, form appropriate, realistic, and clearly communicated expectations, accept the person(s), situations, or events even if we don't agree or understand, and release what no longer belongs to us or isn't our responsibility. This process is foundational to healthy relationships, even if one sided.

Family and Letting Go

Letting go, when it involves family members, can be difficult. Letting go of our adult children is particularly hard for some. Parents and caregivers spend a great deal of time worrying about their children from the day they are born. As the children grow and mature, healthy children start to become independent in their teens in preparation to leave the nest. These are necessary but difficult years. Some adults hold on too tightly and don't grow at the same level as their children. They know they need to let go, but the letting go creates tension. They watch their teens and adult children value things and make confusing choices that don't align with the values they were raised with.

Parents and caregivers may believe they know the choices best for their adult children, and they may. Adult children need to make mistakes, like their parents did. It is essential they sit in the consequences from those decisions. Parents and caregivers, today, are less likely than prior generations to let their adult children experience consequences for their choices. They spend their energy and finances bailing out adult children in all kinds of situations whether it's with money, moving back home, furnishing a car, or more. Many of us know family or friends who struggle with this scenario.

Parents step in primarily because they don't like to see their children "suffer" even if their child is an adult and made unwise or unfortunate decisions. I've had to watch this in my own family. The healthy solution is to let go and allow them to figure out what they need to do. It's hard to watch, but the end result is better in the long run. If parents stay too connected to the situation, resentments will form by both parties. This is tough because there isn't an exact handbook for each situation.

We have a family member with a disability that, thankfully, struggles less now as he's grown farther into adulthood. There were several undiagnosed years we didn't know what to do. It was hard to know when to enter in and when to let go and let him struggle and deal with his own consequences. The process was like a dance, and we frequently stepped on toes.

There were medical issues and living arrangements we needed to help with but were confused about how much we do and what his responsibilities were. I am grateful most of these struggles are in the past and he now makes decisions we previously made for him. It was a long process learning when and how much to let go.

With younger children, most parents and caregivers want to make sure they help their child develop good self-esteem. We have a culture of protecting our children from feeling disappointed, sad, or hurt. We often step in to right the wrong without giving the responsibility to our child. We make sure every child has a trophy, we take them to get a treat when they've had a bad day, we march down to the school when we feel our child's teacher or others have mistreated them, and we buy things to make our children feel better.

As caring as this may sound, it actually prevents children from developing resiliency and invites them to develop manipulation skills. Children need to develop coping skills to face their disappointments and figure out how to do life. What's frequently missing is the parent's letting go.

Healthy parents and caregivers can lovingly detach so their child can figure out solutions to their problems. This builds resiliency. Children who learn resiliency and how to navigate their disappointments are successful in building their self-esteem instead of their caregivers solving their problems for them.

Just as infants need to learn to soothe themselves when they are upset, so do children and adults. We can give words of encouragement, affirming we believe in them, and trust they can solve their own problems, even if they are crying and saying they can't. When we fix our children's problems, we inadvertently send them a message we don't believe they can do it themselves. Resiliency and the ability to problem solve is what builds self-esteem, not the lack of problems or parents unnecessarily "fixing" the child's problem.

We love our family, however, some situations with family members can be difficult to navigate. They keep calling us for help or pull us in a way we feel guilty if we don't do what they want. We feel badly for them, but also taken advantage of. Setting boundaries with our family members is necessary regarding money, time, action, opinions, and other things unique to each family. We may get push back when we initiate these boundaries, but remember we are the ones who teach others how to treat and relate to us. It's up to us, not them, to relate in a relationally healthy way.

We usually can't physically let go of family members, but we can let go of our perceived sense of responsibility for them. Once family members, without disabilities, are past eighteen, no one is responsible for them but themselves. As family, we can be responsible to them, but not for them. Being responsible to someone is when we are kind, thoughtful, and considerate. We are only responsible for someone if they are a minor child or a family member with a disability. If we take on the responsibility for an abled body adult, resentments form on both sides.

We've covered new territory for some, and it may take some time for it to all sink in. My hope is as you process this material, you experience some healthy "ah ha" moments. My deepest desire is that you are able to receive the freedom offered by reading and understanding why "it's me, not you." Let's go forward with our last chapter and learn more about letting go.

Letting Go Reflections are in the Appendix.

Chapter 9
Learn to Let Go

Jason, twenty, just ended his second year of college and told his parents, Lonnie and Jill, he needed a break for at least a semester before he returned back to school. He told them he was going to move into an apartment with an old high school buddy. His parents had some reservations and asked the appropriate questions about his goals and getting a job. Jason answered the questions to their satisfaction.

He moved in with Craig and told his parents he would start looking for a job in about two weeks. He wanted to take a short break. Lonny shared his concerns with Jill. She reassured him that it will all work out.

"Jason worked hard these last two years. He needs a break."

He asked them for money to bridge the gap from starting the job until he got his first paycheck. Craig was asking him to share only the cost of utilities. Lonny and Jill sent Jason enough to cover two months and told him they wouldn't send any more.

As the days passed, Jason's parents occasionally called to see how his job search was going. He described all his attempts to find a job but with no success. At the end of the two months, Jason was still without a job. He asked his parents to give him more money to pay Craig for the rent. This was a huge disappointment for his parents, but they provided the money anyway. They, again, challenged Jason to get a job.

After four more months, Jason still didn't have a job. At the same time, Craig's lease was up and Jason had to find another place to live. With some hesitation, Lonny and Jill said yes to Jason's request to live with them. The three signed a contract that stipulated the terms of Jason's return home.

As is common with these stories, a year later, Jason was still at home and didn't have a job. Tension was building, and Lonny and Jill were tired of their constant prodding. They spoke to a friend who went through something similar with their daughter.

The friend acknowledged the emotional conflict he knew they were going through. He went through it himself. He told them that if there's nothing wrong with Jason psychologically or physically, they need to give Jason an ultimatum and follow through. No more second chances. On their friend's recommendation, they gave Jason the ultimatum. This time they offered a reasonable time frame for Jason to find a job and save for the first two months of rent. They were not going to remind him or nag him.

Jason didn't follow through and Lonny and Jill had to do the hard task of telling Jason he had to find another place to live. Jason was dumbfounded. He apparently never thought his parents would follow through. He became angry and said some hurtful things. He packed his bags and left. He didn't communicate with them for months.

His parents worried about him and tried to find out where he was, but to no avail. They found little comfort in knowing if something bad happened to him, they would be notified by friends or the police. Letting go was extremely difficult.

Stories like this often have happy endings. The son or daughter stays distant for a period of time and then realizes they need to get their act together. They accept they are now in an adult-to-adult relationship with their parents.

Other endings turn out poorly. The son or daughter doesn't have the "ah ha" moment for years and sometimes never does. These parents experience years of emotional suffering. However, some parents are able to affirm themselves the letting go was the healthiest action they could take. Their child is an adult and has to make their own choices. Parents cannot continue to pick up pieces for their adult children, but the results are often heartbreaking. Parents need support through friends, church, community groups, and twelve-step programs.

Knowing when to let go of anything is hard. There isn't an absolute rule book or road map to know when it's time or how to let go. This chapter and the previous chapter were written to help with the struggle. Even in the struggle, there are benefits with our healthy letting go.

Detaching and Healthy Letting Go

Letting go contains elements of detaching which may feel uncomfortable. When I first heard about detaching, it sounded too harsh. I've learned detaching isn't necessarily a negative thing to do. Healthy detaching may seem like it goes against everything we've been taught about being there for others, but it isn't. Healthy detaching simply means we are encouragers, not enablers. When we try to hang onto another's problems, it's usually for unhealthy reasons. Healthy detaching doesn't mean we don't care about someone or something anymore, it means we want our relationships to be healthy and respectful.

When we go through the process of detaching, we may worry others think we don't care or we don't want to help. Detaching is common and goes on our entire life. Relationships ebb and flow. The truth is, detaching and letting go can be the healthiest, most caring, and helpful things we can give those we love. It depends on why we are detaching. Detaching out of anger is not healthy. Detaching because we have to stop enabling is healthy. So, we need make sure we are detaching in a healthy way. Deborah Reber agrees:

"Letting go doesn't mean you don't care about someone anymore. It's just realizing the only person you really have control over is yourself."[xxxi]
-Deborah Reber, Chicken Soup for the Teenage Soul

Assumptions and Letting Go

Mack and Terrance were good friends and teammates. They had many mutual friends and did things together. On one occasion, Mack hung out with some guys and they all went to a movie. Terrance had other obligations and didn't go. A few days later, Terrance overheard some of their friends talking about how Mack was glad Terrance wasn't with them the other night. All Terrance heard was Mack didn't want him around. He started to pull away, and their relationship became strained. Mack was confused by Terrence's distance and decided Terrence wasn't as committed to their friendship as he thought. Over the next few months the strain continued. Nothing improved and within a year, they rarely saw each other.

A few years later, Terrance was still hurt by Mack's words. He wouldn't let it go. His wife offered encouragement and another point of view, but Terrance's hurt and resentment continued. Things would trigger the memory, and he would become sullen.

At their five year reunion, Terrance steered himself to the opposite side of the room from Mack. Other former classmates noticed the situation and approached Terrance. Reluctant to talk, Terrance said a few things, but then clammed up.

Mack decided to approach his friend and asked if they could step outside for a few minutes. Terrance agreed. Outside, Mack asked, "What's wrong?" After a few "nothings," Mack said, "Come on, T, what's going on?"

Terrance told him what he overheard years ago. Mack had trouble placing the timeframe, so Terrance linked it to the time he didn't go to a movie with him and other friends.

"I remember now. There was a fight outside the theater that night. It appeared to be racially charged. It was scary, and I was glad you weren't there to witness it. That's all I meant when I said I was glad you weren't there."

Terrance was dumbfounded. He had no idea Mack's comment was a caring and protective comment. He realized he was the one with the problem. He made assumptions and the assumptions trumped their long-term friendship.

Fortunately, the two were able to make amends, let go of the hurt, and renew their relationship. Assumptions are dangerous and, in this case, almost ruined a friendship forever.

Ruminating and Letting Go

We can torture ourselves by thinking the same things day and night about ourselves, family, friends, things, and events. This repetitive thinking is unproductive except to keep us up at night and create anxiety during the day. Keeping our thoughts under control is hard. One reason it's hard is some believe thinking about it over and over is "doing" something to help solve a problem. Or, as in the *Acceptance* chapter, fear or misunderstandings are often the root of our overthinking. We want the security of being in the know but analyzing and overthinking doesn't provide it. They just create more anxiety.

There is a story, told by many, about two monks. This version comes from Eckhart Tolle[xxxii], a spiritual teacher.

"Tanzan and Ekido were walking along a country road that had become extremely muddy after heavy rains. Near a village, they came upon a young woman who was trying to cross the road, but the mud was so deep it would have ruined the silk kimono she was wearing. Tanzan at once picked her up and carried her to the other side. The monks walked on in silence. Five hours later, as they were approaching the lodging temple, Ekido couldn't restrain himself any longer.

'Why did you carry that girl across the road?' he asked. 'We monks are not supposed to do things like that.'

'I put the girl down hours ago,' said Tanzan. 'Are you still carrying her?'"

Ekido was apparently pondering the situation for five hours. What good did it do for him? Was he feeling resentful? Did he feel like his brother monk, Tanzan, needed to be reported? Did he worry about the consequences? Did he ruminate the woman might expose them or misinterpret the gesture? One monk chose to let go, the other continued to ruminate and hang on.

As we have discussed before, what good comes from overthinking and ruminating? Does it solve problems? Perhaps ten percent of the time. More often, it causes anxiety, irritation, unreasonable demands, lack of sleep, and feelings of helplessness. We know we need to stop, but can't seem to do it. When I get stuck in my overthinking, I say to myself, "Don't go there, girl. Don't go there." If you pick up what you let go of, look at it, smile, tell it that it no longer belongs to you, and then toss it into the sea.

What type of thoughts do you continually think about and can't seem to control? Are they about you or are they about others? It depends on what it's about. My thoughts usually go to wondering if I said or did something wrong, fairness and justice issues, being misunderstood, and how do I fix this?

Overthinking and analyzing are negative approaches and hinder problem solving even though we believe our thinking can solve problems. I know I need to let go of my ruminating, but it can be hard, at times. When letting go, we come face to face with the realization all this replaying, analyzing, planning, and plotting is not helpful. It's harmful and annoying. Overthinking is like a dripping faucet or being on a merry-go-round you can't get off. Below are some tips for reducing our overthinking and over analyzing:

-Journal.

-Speak gratitudes out loud to calm yourself.

-Live in acceptance.

-Let go and surrender your thoughts to God.

-Go for a walk or a swim.

-Remember our way is just "a" way, not "the" way.

-Do something nice for someone.

-Read scripture like Philippians 4:4-13.

-Eliminate all sentences that start with "what if" and "if only."

-Don't let negative thoughts take up space in your brain.

-Call a friend – not to complain, but to discuss positive things.

-Spend time thinking about your own business, not someone else's.

-Write out a worse-case scenario and see if the results are manageable.

-Identify the actual fear, allow twenty minutes to mull it over it, then let go.

-Recognize there are many different ways to accomplish something.

-Walk outside and look up at the sky. Know there is a bigger picture out there.

-Center yourself - notice what is going on around you. Stay in the present moment.

The Past and Letting Go

Some of us may say or believe we've already let go of resentments and expectations and are living in acceptance. We explain, "All that's in the past. I've put it away. It's over." Putting it away and stating "it's over" may not be letting go. Our body remembers everything, and deciding in our heads we've let go of things in the past doesn't necessarily remove it from our body. If it's not removed, healed, or forgiven, it's still inside. The past shows up at times when we or others are puzzled over our unusual reactions or non-reactions to things. It shows up when we become emotional over something insignificant or have unexplained pain in our body.

When this happens, it's usually because we haven't fully healed or released what's in our body. We believe we are over it and don't need to do anything else. However, it's still there and releases itself somewhere and at unexpected times and in unexpected ways. I call it "leaking out." It leaks out at times through tears, laughter, anger, pain, depression, dreams, or anxiety. Just because we don't dwell on something anymore doesn't mean we've let it go.

Has this happened to you? It happened to me. After my father died, I couldn't cry. Tears would try to come but wouldn't. As time went on, I thought I was disrespecting him because I hadn't cried. I did have some "watery eyes," but no out-right crying. I didn't understand this, he was my rock.

The reason I didn't cry may have been because I had so much on my plate. At the funeral home, when we were making his arrangements, I was pacing back and forth waiting for a phone call.

A phone call telling me when a specialist, in another state, could see my husband and I for our marriage problems. I couldn't tell my family what was going on. Not, while we are planning my father's funeral.

I may not have been able to cry because I just couldn't cope with losing my dad and my husband at the same time. I went from home to husband. I had no idea how to be a single woman. Years continued to pass. It took about fifteen years for it to happen. I was casually opening a Christmas card from a long-time friend. Inside the card were pictures of my dad's funeral at Arlington Cemetery. She wanted me to have them. That was it. I broke down. I sobbed and sobbed. The grief was always in my body. It finally came out. What a relief. I was so happy. I finally cried for my dad, and it was a full-blown cry.

If you are concerned because you haven't cried or become appropriately emotional, ask a close, safe relative or friend if they're aware of something you need to let go of. Ask the Lord to reveal anything you aren't healed from or haven't let go of. As we learned in the resentment chapter, journal about what you are still holding on to. Use your own handwriting. Remember, when thoughts come from our heart or mind and continue down our arm and onto paper, more is revealed than if we just think about it or use a keyboard to write them out.

We are often surprised at what shows up on paper. There's revelation, healing, insight, and comfort in this process. Journaling has been a life saver for me at times. Worry, sadness, and disappointment are minimized when I journal. Below is an encouraging scripture from Hebrews 12:1.

"Therefore, since we are surrounded by such a great cloud of witnesses, let us throw off everything that hinders and the sin that so easily entangles, and let us run with perseverance the race marked out for us."

The Why's and Letting Go

Many of us get stuck in the "why." It's natural to want to know why, but the "whys" can create problems. The whys can stop us from letting go. "Why didn't I get the job?" "Why did she do that to me?" "Why can't I have_____ or be like_____?" "Why did it happen?" "Why didn't it happen?" The accurate answer is we may not need to know why. The "whys" can consume us. Sometimes we never find out why.

It's healthy to seek good counsel, journal, or read books and articles in order to let go of our whys. Sometimes the why becomes apparent years later. Sometimes not. It's our job to live in acceptance. It's our job to let go. At this point, it is what it is.

I love what Joel Osteen[xxxiii], a pastor, speaker, and author in Houston, Texas, said about this. He suggested we put the "why" in a file called "I don't understand it" and then leave it alone. He also illustrates this point by saying, "Don't put a question mark where God put a period."

When I get stuck in the whys, I visualize a back burner or a top shelf. The back burner is turned off, and the top shelf is not easy to reach. Whys sit there until God brings the problem to the front burner or the bottom shelf. Then it's time for me to address it. In the interim, I leave it alone. This eliminates my need to ruminate or overthink the situation. The problem will stay where it is until I need to address it.

Surrendering

Surrendering is also a key element in letting go. The word surrender can sound ominous, but it's part of the pathway to freedom. When we surrender to what is true about our situations, we live in acceptance instead of discontent. Acceptance is also letting go of who and where we want others to be. We trust the larger picture instead of what we want the picture to look like. Surrendering releases unrealistic expectations of ourselves and others. It's letting go and living by the picture God painted for our life, not the picture we've painted for our life. I like this visual. I image the picture God painted for me, and I try to stay in His picture.

Thinking about the word "surrender" can create an uncomfortable feeling because we imagine we'll lose control. The truth is we've never had control. Control is an illusion. The desire for control is normal, but it can undo us. We focus on how we see things, or want people or things to be, rather than accepting what is. Lack of control feels scary, but there are great benefits.

Surrendering is full of unexpected blessings. We take our hands and minds off things. We are set free, and the door opens to receive help and confirmation from unexpected sources.

Several commercials, over the years, show different scenes of active people becoming hot and sweaty. They find relief by drinking various ice-cold drinks. The commercials emphasize how drinking an ice-cold drink is like falling or jumping, without a care, into a swimming pool. There is always a big splash, the sign of relief. These commercials are symbolic to me. It's a perfect picture of surrender. Falling or jumping into a pool, without a care, is like falling into God's arms and receiving his plans for us. What a relief!

Forgiveness and Letting Go

Forgiveness and letting go are buddies. They go hand in hand. Some circumstances make it hard to let go. It does take strength and willpower to let go. This strength can move us into new places. We are free to choose whether these new places represent freedom and opportunity or whether we continue to pass freedom by and carry a ball and chain around? I am not minimizing hurts, sorrows, abuse, or betrayals. They are legitimate pains we experience. It means healing, forgiveness, and letting go are hard. What I suggest is do this process in parts. We can heal and let go in parts. It doesn't have to be all or nothing.

Think of a wound or difficulty you have. Is someone responsible for creating it? Are other wounds attached to it? If so, does it continue to get bigger, and does the bandage keep coming off? If it's grown too big, it may be hard to let go of it all at once. Break it down into parts and let go of each part in your own timing.

Sometimes we've experienced pain for so long, our identity is attached to it. Part of us wants it to go away and part of us doesn't. Sometimes we say, "This is just the way it is, nothing can be done." We've decided being a victim is okay. The way to get out of this is to understand the way we think influences the way we feel. If we think like a victim, we will feel like a victim.

I took a class for my continuing education credits call "Changing How We Feel by Changing How We Think" presented by the Institute for Brain Potential of Arlington, Texas[xxxiv]. The title tells it all. Review in chapter 3 how Jorge used this method to reframe his frustrating day at work.

The other day I looked at my calendar and didn't think I could do it all. I started complaining internally that I just needed a break. My day felt gray. Then I remembered I needed to reword what I was thinking. I landed on "This day is full, but I trust that I will be okay and I might learn something new." Internally, my gray day lifted, and the sun was shining again. Watch your thoughts, they can determine your day, how you feel, and how you relate to others. Let go of discouraging thoughts and replace them with genuine optimist thoughts.

When I decide to let go or to forgive, how I process it makes a difference. There are times I wonder, if I do let go or forgive, will I lose my power or pass it over to someone? Will I become less than? This thinking is not healthy. Forgiving and passing power to someone are in two different worlds. Our forgiving is our forgiving. Remember, "it's me, not you." There's no passing our power to someone else. We are our own entity.

Other good questions are: Is it demeaning to let go? Is letting go allowing someone to get off scot free? Is letting go giving up or giving in? I respond to these questions with: Letting go is not giving up. Letting go is intentional. Giving up is giving up.

Resisting Forgiveness

Unforgiveness is toxic. We may feel someone doesn't deserves forgiveness. This isn't our place to decide. God is the judge. Unforgiveness keeps us hooked to our pain like an addiction. We may feel justified for staying in unforgiveness, but it only hurts us. We've all been around people who only see the negative side of things. Watch out for this negativity. Reframe it.

Unforgiveness has no ending point. It goes on and on and on. There're times we don't want to forgive because we've become used to living as a victim or martyr. We may secretly like the drama or blaming our situation on someone else. Then, we don't have to do any personal work.

A difficult part of letting go is the cause of our situation or heart ache may be at the hands of someone else. If true, how we process it and live with it is still our responsibility. I'm going to say that again as it is extremely important. Even though the cause of our situation may be at the hands of someone else, how we process it and live with it is our responsibility.

We know the right thing to do is to let go and forgive, but we don't want to. We pray about it, but our heart doesn't catch up. Be kind to yourself. Forgive yourself. Just because we forgive someone doesn't mean we have to continue or reestablish a relationship with them. People may ask you, "Why haven't you gotten over this?" You do not have to give them an answer.

Keep working on it. God knows your heart, and if you truly desire to forgive and let go, he will help you get there. He is an amazing God, and you are His creation. Let's see what the founder of Moody Bible Institute says about this:

"Let God have your life;
He can do more with it than you can."[xxxv]
-Dwight L. Moody, American evangelist

Letting Them off the Hook?

Sometimes I don't want to consider acceptance and forgiveness because I'm afraid I'm letting someone get away with something. The Psalmist gives us good advice about this concern.

"Do not fret because of evil men or those who do wrong; for like the grass they will soon wither, like green plants they will soon die away. Trust in the Lord and do good; dwell in the land and enjoy safe pasture." Psalm 37:1-4.

I love the word "enjoy." Enjoy safe pasture. What a peaceful picture. Verse 4 in the Message (MSG) translation of the Bible says, "Keep company with God, get in on the best." When we forgive and let go, we are freeing ourselves from a heavy burden and allowing ourselves to "enjoy safe pasture" and are "getting in on the best."

Jesus told us to forgive seventy times seven. He doesn't say or imply we need to let someone "get a pass." He says just "do it, forgive." He is the judge of all and will take care of the rest.

The good news is the Bible has many examples of people letting go of people, things, and events so they can live surrendered to what God wants for them. To be able to let go, acceptance and forgiveness are key. It may be difficult to consider forgiveness because we believe someone won't suffer the consequences they should face. We aren't letting them off the hook, we're letting God do the justice part. Unforgiveness keeps us hooked, and unforgiveness gives us permission to stay living in the "yuck" or drama. Does that sound like something desirable, something we want?

Remember, hurting people hurt people. Having compassion for our offender is difficult but freeing. If we're able to muster up some compassion, healing becomes less heavy and creates a healthy release within us. This isn't to excuse harmful behaviors; it's about adjusting how we view our offender. We have the power to release ourselves from this burden. It's how we process our situation that makes the difference. We don't have to wait on anyone else to do or not do something. Again, "it's me, not you."

This is the foundation of this book. When we realize we have the power to change things within us, we don't have to wait on anyone. It's all about how we process it and whether we stay in the "blame" mode or the "freedom" mode.

This excerpt from the *Language of Letting Go*, December 4, by Melody Beattie[xxxvi] hits the nail on the head:

> "Letting go means we acknowledge that hanging on so tightly isn't helping to solve the problem, change the person, or get the outcome we desire. It isn't helping us. In fact, we learn that hanging on often blocks us from getting what we want and need."

"Hanging on" are good descriptive words. Are you hanging on to something and don't feel you can let go? Why? Is it helping you or keeping a hotspot in you? I've experienced people hanging on and not realizing they were. Hanging on can be what continues to trigger us and keeps us from moving forward.

Solomon in Ecclesiastics 3:1-7 echoes the same idea, but in a familiar poetic way:

> "There is a time for everything and a season for every activity under the heavens: a time to be born and a time to die, a time to plant and a time to uproot, a time to kill and a time to heal, a time to tear down and a time to build, a time to weep and a time to laugh, a time to mourn and a

time to dance, a time to scatter stones and a time to gather them, a time to embrace and a time to refrain from embracing, a time to search and a time to give up, a time to keep and a time to throw away, a time to tear and a time to mend, a time to be silent and a time to speak."

True Freedom

Oh, the freedom available to us with forgiveness and letting go! There are many stories of ordinary people doing the extraordinary by forgiving and letting go of what some consider unforgivable things. They decided they won't be defined by their situation or by unforgiveness. They chose REAL freedom and their story has given them REAL influence in all their relationships. The scripture below says it all.

> "Get rid of all bitterness, rage and anger, brawling and slander, along with every form of malice. Be kind and compassionate to one another, forgiving each other just as Christ God forgave you" (Ephesians 4:31).

Earlier I shared how Chris deeply hurt me and how I wanted Chris to know how deep the hurt was and how Melody Beattie's *Language of Letting Go* helped me let go of that need.

Years later, I struggled wondering whether I'd forgiven Chris. I wanted to forgive, but never felt I did, even though I said the right words. My pastor at the time, Reverend Jim Welch, gave a sermon about forgiveness. At first, it seemed to be an average sermon on forgiveness. Then he said something I never heard before. I was riveted in my seat because what he said sounded like I could finally be certain I forgave Chris. He said, something close to, "Forgiveness is not forgetting or not feeling the pain. True forgiveness is cancelling the debt." I never heard it put this way before – "canceling the debt."

"Oh! I can do this! I can do this!" I wanted to jump out of my seat. I was finally free. The struggle was over, the debt was cancelled. The enemy can't whisper negativity about my unforgiveness anymore. Chris is forgiven. I have cancelled the debt. I'm free.

Clara Barton[xxxvii], who founded the Red Cross, was asked about someone who hurt her. Her response was "I distinctly remember forgetting that hurt."

If you've been wounded, like most of us have, grieve your loss, take the appropriate and necessary action, set boundaries, and release your offender. Many of us are unable to release our offender all at once. If the relationship is a family member or close friend, forgiving and letting go is difficult and may have to be done in stages. Cognitively we can say we are forgiving, and that's a good place to start. Get started, and eventually your heart will allow full forgiveness.

As recorded in Proverbs 19:1:

"A man's wisdom gives him patience; it is to his glory to overlook an offense."

It is tough to let go, but it's the healthy thing to do. Your life is less cluttered and your anxiety is reduced. The REAL benefit is your freedom.

Moving On

We've seen why letting go is important, because it moves us into the freedom we've longed for and were created for. It keeps our relationships healthy. It gives us freedom to move along in our personal and spiritual growth. The freedom that allows us to grow closer to God and others. This freedom redirects us to focus on what we need to be looking at, thinking about, and responding to.

Letting go doesn't mean you don't care about someone or something anymore. It can be a form of detaching in love. It's also realizing the only thing we truly have control over is ourselves, right here, right now. Letting go is a necessary process of adapting to the ever-changing realities of life – leaving behind the past to make way for the present. It's also part of living in acceptance and not camping out in the "I wish" – "I wish it were this," "I wish it were that." Letting go counters the heaviness that enters our lives for many different reasons. We can remind ourselves, "I'm not going to let someone or something determine how I feel for the rest of my life."

REAL Influence™ and *It's Me, Not You* are part of the spiritual and emotional foundations for healthy relationships. Letting go and forgiveness allow us to grow closer to God, ourselves, and others. They support building healthy relationships whether at home, work, or in our community. This freedom allows us to direct our thought processes to what we need to be looking at, thinking about, and responding to.

We're ready to live in REAL freedom with REAL influence and enjoy healthy relationships. Freedom without resentments and bitterness. Freedom with realistic and managed expectations. Freedom by living in acceptance instead of resistance. Freedom by letting go and cancelling debts. Freedom by letting go of the obstacles preventing us from living emotionally and spiritually free. Let's review those key strategies that contribute to developing and keeping healthy relationships by letting go:

-Make the decision to forgive. Do it in parts.

-Cancel our offender's debt.

-Forgive ourselves.

-Release our overthinking and analyzing. Rest instead.

-Trust the larger picture, not just the picture in front of us.

-Fall back and surrender to the Lord's loving care.

-Reject the spirit of discontent.

-Pray a blessing on those you feel anger or resentment toward.

-Focus on our blessings not our stressors or mistakes.

-Live in acceptance of who we are and who others are.

-Remember God sees the bigger picture, we see the smaller picture.

-Pray the St. Francis of Assisi Prayer:

Lord, make me an instrument of your peace. Where there is hatred, let me bring love.

Where there is injury, let me bring pardon. Where there is doubt, let me bring faith.

Where there is despair, let me bring hope. Where there is darkness, let me bring light.

Where there is sadness, let me bring joy. O Divine Master, grant that I may not so much seek to be consoled, as to console; To be understood, as to understand; To be loved, as to love.

For it is in giving that we receive. It is in pardoning that we are pardoned, and it is in dying that we are born to Eternal Life. Amen.[xxxviii]

When we accept that "it's me, not you," we have a choice to live REAL, with REAL freedom and have REAL influence in our relationships. We aren't waiting on anyone else. We feel lighter and more alive. We sleep better at night and don't take things personally. We trust ourselves to make healthier decisions in our relationships. We see things with a different perspective, a healthy perspective.

Releasing **R**esentments, evaluating **E**xpectations, acquiring **A**cceptance, and **L**etting go moves us into action, problem solving, and gratitude. Knowing "it's me, not you," "it's us, not them," gives us the freedom we need to control our actions, thinking, and feelings. We are in charge of how we relate to ourselves and others. We now have tools to experience healthy relationships and a healthy spiritual life. It is worth it. It's freedom! Let's celebrate!

Learn to Let Go Reflections are in the Appendix.

Appendix

Chapter Reflections Questions

It's Me, Not You Reflections

1.What did you hope to gain by reading *It's Me, Not You?* What was the result?

2. Why do we need to focus on ourselves for the changes we want?

      a. What changes do you need to do?

      b. What is going to be difficult?

3. What is your part in healing and creating healthy relationships?

4. Is there someone you trust to talk to about this?

5. Is there a quote or quotes in this chapter you want to remember and might be a good mantra for you? If so, write about it here.

6. Read Ephesians 4. What additional wisdom did you gain from this chapter?

7. What do you want to work on first, then second?

Resentments Reflections

1. Before reading about resentments, did you know how harmful they are and the damage they do? What are the dangers for you, personally, to hold onto anger and resentments?

2. Do you have resentments because of some assumptions you made? What are they?

3. What was the set-up in the story about Abraham and Sarah in Genesis 16:1-15?

    a. What created the resentments and bitterness?

    b. Did Sarah or Abraham take responsibility for them?

4. Do the verses in Hebrews 12:14-15 say we can't disagree with people?

    a. What is the spirit of these verses when it comes to disagreements with others?

    b. Does the other person(s) have to make "every effort?"

5. Do you have trouble saying "yes" or "no?" What have you learned to do?

6. Read Psalm 116 for personal encouragement.

Releasing Resentments Reflections

1. Does releasing and preventing resentments make more sense now?

    a. What steps are you going to take?

    b. What successes have you had?

2. How does James 3:9-17 relate to releasing resentments? What is James trying to tell us to do instead?

3. What is God's role found in Psalm 50:6, 75:7, Hebrews 12:23-24, and James 4:11-12? How do these verses apply to our resentments and attitudes toward others?

4. What did you learn about the *shoulds*?

5. How can you implement keeping "short accounts?"

6. What other choices do you have than resentments?

7. Can you take the action needed?

8. Journal about the shift you made.

Expectations Reflections

1. What problems do unspoken expectations, by you or others, create in your life?

2. What expectations do you have about God, your family, friends, and co-workers?

3. What secret contracts do you make or others make for you?

4. Sometimes we don't want to communicate our expectation to others. Why?

5. Luke 10:38-40 describes a situation that happens every day. Do you think Martha or Mary clearly communicated their expectations to each other? Were there some secret contracts?

6. Describe some scenes in your life resembling the situation with Martha and Mary.

7. Many expectations come from our perspectives and values. How are you going to use this information for your good and for others?

8. Are you disappointed about an unmet expectation that still bothers you? How can you prevent this unmet expectation from becoming a resentment?

Evaluate Expectations Reflections

1. Did the "a" way and "the" way section help you?

    a. How?

    b. What is one of your "the way" that needs to change to an "a way."

2. What else did you learn about the *shoulds*?

3. How are you going to implement problem solving in your relationships?

4. What did you learn to prevent the spirit of discontent from entering in?

5. What are legitimate expectations and what are healthy expectations? Are they the same?

6. Evaluate the expectations you have for your relationships. Ask yourself these questions:

a. Have you clearly communicated your expectation or have you fallen into the trap of they *should* know?

b. Is your happiness or sense of well-being dependent on your expectations of others? What would it cost you to adjust this expectation?

Acceptance Reflections

1. Were you surprised acceptance doesn't mean we have to agree or condone?

2. What did you learn about reality and acceptance?

3. How does Colossians 3:12-14 support healthy acceptance of others?

4. Did the information on shame help you? How?

5. Does it work to try and change people? Have you tried or are you trying right how?

    a. Are you successful?

    b. What does this author suggest instead?

6. Read 2 Peter 1:10-11. Do you worry about whether God accepts you? What do you need to confirm?

7. What do you need to work on to accept God, yourself, others, events, or certain situations?

Acquire Acceptance Reflections

1. Has anything shifted in your understanding of acceptance? Write your reflections.

2. Matthew 5:1-12 is home to the Beatitudes. These verses are full of acceptance messages and can be called the "Be Attitudes." What changes do you need to make based on these verses?

3. The Bible has many stories of resistance. It starts at the very beginning with Adam and Eve. Genesis 2-3:9.

    a. Why did Adam and Eve accept Satan's words and resist God's command?

    b. Why did they rationalize their actions?

4. Is there anything you have rationalized recently that indicates your resistance? Instead of reacting with resistance or complaining, according to the Apostle Paul in Philippians 2:14, how should we conduct ourselves?

5. Can you change your resistance to your true emotion such as sad, disappointed, confused, or another emotion?

6. What does "when we live in acceptance, it actually gives us more choices" mean to you?

Letting Go Reflections

1. Do you need to let go of someone or something? Have you built a cage? If so, what's next?

2. Does it seem hard or not fair to let go? Explain.

3. Why is letting go of expectations, assumptions, and some relationships important?

4. In Romans 7:6, what can we let go of because of our faith in Christ? What benefit is it to us?

5. The hope we have through Christ is our salvation and eternal life. It couldn't have happened unless he "let go." What did he let go of? Matthew 26:36-39, 42.

6. In Isaiah 43:18-19, what is Isaiah telling us to do and what hope is he giving us?

7. Can you focus on your blessings and let go of your stressors and mistakes?

8. Write a promise to yourself of something you will let go of.

Learn to Let Go Reflections

1. Look at what you wanted to let go. Is it still the same? Have you added anything more?

2. What obstacles prevent you from letting go or forgiving certain people, things, or events?

3. Is overthinking or ruminating an obstacle? How do you let go? Is it hard for you?

4. What do you need to let go of and give to God? 1 Peter 5:7.

5. What does Paul say about others' business in 1 Thessalonians 4:11 and 1 Peter 4:15?

6. Why is letting go so hard? What is Paul challenging us to let go of in Galatians 5:1? Are you afraid of letting someone off the hook?

7. Is letting go giving up or is it moving on? What is letting go to you? Find a scripture to hold on to and put it in a place to remind you that letting go is freedom.

8. After you let go, what do you need to put in its place, as in Ephesians 4:31-32?

Citations/References

Endnotes

Introduction

[i] Gandhi, Mohandas Karamchand, and Anand T. Hingorani. *The Encyclopaedia of Gandhian Thoughts*. New Delhi: All India Congress Committee, 1985.

[ii] *Public Papers of the Presidents of the United States: Jimmy Carter, 1978, Volume 2a Part 1*. Best Books On Corporation, 2013.

[iii] Roosevelt, Theodore. *Theodore Roosevelt on Bravery: Lessons from the Most Courageous Leader of the Twentieth Century*. New York: Skyhorse Publishing, 2015.

Chapter 1

[iv] "TOP 42 Albert Schweitzer Quotes." Christian Quotes, June 6, 2020. https://www.quoteschristian.com/albert-schweitzer.html.

[v] Churchill, Winston S. "The Gift of a Common Tongue." The International Churchill Society, September 6, 1943. https://winstonchurchill.org/resources/speeches/1941-1945-war-leader/the-price-of-greatness-is-responsibility/.

[vi] Dorjeduck. "Blaming Others ~ 14th Dalai Lama." Just Dharma Quotes, December 7, 2016. https://quotes.justdharma.com/blaming-others/

[vii] *Samuel Smiles': Self-Help*. Petaling Jaya, Selangor: Advantage Quest Publications, 2015.

[viii] Ephesian 4 pp.5-7

Chapter 2

[viv] "Saint Augustine Quotes." BrainyQuote. Xplore. Accessed March 8, 2021. https://www.brainyquote.com/quotes/saint_augustine_384531.

[x] Plato, and Francis Macdonald Cornford. *The Republic of Plato, Translated with Introduction and Notes by Francis Macdonald Cornford*. New York and London: Oxford University Press, 1941.

[xi] "Ann Landers Quote." AZ Quotes. Accessed January 9, 2021. https://www.azquotes.com/quote/413479.

[xii] "Bob Newhart - Stop It - YouTube." n.d. Www.Youtube.com. Accessed December 16, 2020. https://www.youtube.com/watch?v=arPCE3zDRg4.

[xiii] Melody Beattie. *Codependent No More*, Center City Minnesota, Hazelden, 1986.

[xiv] Brewer, D. *Quotes of Mahatma Gandhi, a Words of Wisdom Collection Book*. LULU Pres, Inc, 2019.

Chapter 3

[xv] Carnegie, Dale. *How to Stop Worrying and Start Living*. New York, NY: Simon and Schuster, 1984.

[xvi] King, Martin Luther, Raphael G. Warnock, and Coretta Scott King. *A Gift of Love: Sermons from Strength to Love and Other Preachings*. Boston, MA: Beacon Press, 2012.

[xvii] "Resent Somebody." Oblates of St. Benedict, March 8, 2010. Accessed January 08, 2021. https://oblatesosbbelmont.org/2010/03/16/resent-somebody/.

Chapter 4

[xviii] Sanderson, Brandon. *The Stormlight Archive. the Way of Kings*. New York: Tor, 2011.

Chapter 5

[xviv] Churchill, Winston S. *Churchill By Himself*. New York, NY: Rosetta Books, 2013.

xx Peale, Norman Vincent, and Ruth Stafford Peale. *Discovering the Power of Positive Thinking*. New Delhi, India: Orient Paperbacks, 2006.

Chapter 6

xxi Tracy, Brian. "The Greatest Gift That You Can Give to Others Is the Gift of Unconditional Love and Acceptance." Twitter. Twitter, January 7, 2015. https://twitter.com/BrianTracy/status/552872963201331201.

xxii Raab, Scott. "What I've Learned: Michael J. Fox." Esquire. Esquire, August 21, 2020. https://www.esquire.com/entertainment/interviews/a4045/michaeljfox0108/

xxiii "George Orwell Quote." AZ Quotes. Accessed January 9, 2021. https://www.azquotes.com/quote/221216.

Chapter 7

xxiv Jung, C. G. *Collected Works of C.G. Jung: The First Complete English Edition of the Works of C.G. Jung*. London, UK: Routledge, 1973.

xxv Longfellow, Henry Wadsworth. *Longfellow Day by Day*. Edited by Ann Harris Smith. New York, NY: T.Y. Crowell & Co, 1906.

xxvi Niebuhr, Reinhold, and Robert McAfee Brown. *The Essential Reinhold Niebuhr: Selected Essays and Addresses*. New Haven, CT: Yale University Press, 2009.

Chapter 8

xxvii Landers, Ann. *Wake up and Smell the Coffee!: Advice, Wisdom, and Uncommon Good Sense*. New York, NY: Villard, 1996.

xxviii Bilchik, Nadia. "Opinion: A White South African's Memories of Mandela." CNN. Cable News Network, June 18, 2013. https://www.cnn.com/2013/06/14/opinion/bilchik-nelson-mandela/index.html.

xxviv Beattie, Melody. *The Language of Letting Go: Daily Meditations for Codependents*. New York, NY: HarperCollins, 1993.

xxx https://www.essentialcslewis.com/2015/11/14/ccslq-12-monkey-bars/ "C. S. Lewis Quote." AZ Quotes. Accessed November 17, 2020. https://www.azquotes.com/quote/481078.

Chapter 9

xxxi Canfield, Jack, Deborah Reber, and Mark Victor Hansen. *Chicken Soup for the Teenage Soul: The Real Deal Challenges*. New York, NY: Scholastic, 2006.

xxxii Tolle, Eckhart. *A New Earth: Awakening to Your Life's Purpose*. New York, NY: Penguin Books, 2016.

xxxiii Osteen, Joel. "Don't Waste Your Pain - Joel Osteen." Sermons Online. Sermons Online, March 30, 2020. https://sermons-online.org/joel-osteen/don-t-waste-your-pain-joel-osteen-9-2-2016.

xxxiv "Changing How We Feel by Changing How We Think" "Institute for Brain Potential." 2020. Ibpceu.com. 2020. https://www.ibpceu.com/.

xxxv Dorsett, Lyle W. *A Passion for Souls The Life of D.L. Moody*. Chicago, IL: Moody Publishers, 2003.

xxxvi Beattie, Melody. "Letting Go." Melody Beattie, October 31, 2018. https://melodybeattie.com/letting-go-2/.

xxxvii Rosenvold, Susan. "Discovering Clara Barton: No Ordinary Courage," July 25, 2013. http://discoveringclarabarton.blogspot.com/2013/07/.

xxxviii ThoughtCo. "The Prayer of Saint Francis of Assisi." Learn Religions. https://www.learnreligions.com/prayer-of-saint-francis-of-assisi-542575 (accessed December 16, 2020).

Photo Credits

Cover Photos

Front Cover

Blue sky with clouds; Krystine Kercher 2015; used by permission; Lincoln Nebraska

Petrified wood rock; Krystine Kercher 2012; used by permission; Lincoln Nebraska

Men climbers help each other in the mountains; photo by Prazisss 2018; used by permission of DepositPhotos; Ukraine Dnepropetrovsk

Back Cover

Blue sky with clouds; Krystine Kercher 2015; used by permission; Lincoln Nebraska

Petrified wood rock; Krystine Kercher 2012; used by permission; Lincoln Nebraska

Author photo; Aja Vickers 2021; used by permission; Houston Texas

ABOUT THE AUTHOR

Laura McPherson, MS, LPC, LMFT is a licensed professional counselor and licensed marriage and family therapist. She speaks at conferences, retreats and individual events. Laura is passionate about helping others improve their relationships with families, friends and co-workers. When relationships improve, anxiety and depression are reduced. She developed the REAL formula to help others attain and keep healthy relationships.

CPSIA information can be obtained
at www.ICGtesting.com
Printed in the USA
LVHW112354010621
689062LV00005B/145